Levin J. Allen
Pittsburgh, PA
412-512-9375
Levinallen@icloud.com

The Art of IT Service Management

(ITサービス管理の法)

A concise and holistic focus on Quality within IT Service Management

Levin J. Allen

Pittsburgh, PA

ISBN 13: 978-0-692-07380-3 (Paperback)
ISBN 10: 0-692-07380-9

Cover Photography by Levin J. Allen.
Book design by Levin J. Allen.

Printed in the United States of America.

First printing, 2018.

Publisher: Levin/Allen United States
Pittsburgh, PA, 15145

Dedication

This book is dedicated to anyone who has been forced to make the decision to leave a company because of poor management, indistinct leadership, or bad culture and desires to create or be part of something better.

I'd also like to express my deepest appreciation and respect to 4 Leaders that I have had the pleasure of working with during my career who have left a lasting influence on me and how I manage today due to their professionalism, focus, diligence, rectitude, and trust:

- Richard Moore
- Chris Kowalski
- Bob Knutson
- Dr. Brian Miller

Your influence has help to make me the confident, wise, and honorable manager and director that I am today.

どうもありがとうございました

"Strive not to be a success, but rather to be of value."

-Albert Einstein

Table of Contents

Levin J. Allen

PREFACE

Given the critical importance of the IT manager within most companies, the fact that it is a cornerstone role for client, staff, and company interests, and can be a point of either positive or negative impact on service delivery, client satisfaction, and staff retention, I have written this book in hopes of sharing my insights, experiences, and research regarding IT Service Management. My hope is that it may hold some value for current or aspiring managers as well as with upper management and leadership personnel who are responsible for hiring for these positions. The goal is to highlight certain useful, helpful, and in some cases critical elements and considerations related to service management in general and specific to the IT service management arena. The overall objectives are to help with the retention of valuable staff, maintain and retain satisfied clients, and subsequently lend to company profitability and stability. I hope that you find this book to be concise and informative, as well as a commonsense guide for IT service management.

– Levin J. Allen

FORWARD

Levin J. Allen
The Art of IT Service Management

This book represents a compilation of insights from 15 years of experience within the field of IT service management, formal training in information technology, and certifications in six sigma and ITIL. I also leverage my familiarity with other quality management methodologies, tools, and best practices and reference my personal observations and experiences. Within this book I examine common and recurring themes regarding both issues and successes relating to client satisfaction, staff engagement, and IT service performance as well as other elements relating to service delivery, service support, company profitability, quality management, and continuous improvement efforts.

First and foremost, I feel that it is important to mention that no matter where you are with regards to quality management within your area of management, there are 2 vital facts to consider: (a) that there is always both room for, and a continuing need for, improvement over time and (b) there are dozens of very well vetted, developed, and implemented methodologies, tools, ideologies, and philosophies specifically focused on quality management, operational control, continuous improvement, and overall management of performance with regards to service delivery and support. As I will mention more in depth within this book, what is perceived as quality today by whoever your client or customer base may be, may not be perceived as the same level of quality tomorrow. This is due to innovative ideas and solutions becoming commonplace over time, competition building a 'better mousetrap' that becomes the de facto/current standard for quality, changes in technology that become the outriggers for creativity and innovation, and the human predilection to become delighted by that which is new, different, more beneficial, or overall perceived as being more valuable.

Over the years, with exposure to the above-mentioned considerations as well as study and actual application of some of the more prominent methodologies, philosophies, and tools it has become apparent to me that there are:

> *Overlapping "core considerations" that can be found with regards to the oversight and management of quality and control going as far back as Sun Tzu's treatise 'The Art of War' and reaching all the way to modern day revisions for ITIL, ISO 9001:2015, Six Sigma, TQM, ITSM, and with other leading best practices and guiding principles.*

> *Reoccurring common mistakes and oversights that companies can and do make regarding IT management that can, and often do, negatively impact staff, clients, and even the company's wellbeing.*

If during your management career you have not been exposed to or have not had the opportunity to study many of the leading IT quality management offerings and best practices, this book is an attempt to:

- Offer my insights and experiences, which may help you to quickly accumulate beneficial insight vicariously

- Place your focus on the common beneficial themes shared across most current day best practices and tools in order for you to focus your attention on the 'universally best' concepts, methodologies, philosophies, and best practices from various leading authors and organizations without needing to perform a deep dive into all of them

- Introduce you to some of the most beneficial and informative, (or at least enlightening) methods, guidelines, and principles in hopes that you may find some of use personally or useful to your company, by way of a quick introduction to them

I will take a moment to mention at this point that although the focus of this book is mainly towards IT managers and their roles and responsibilities within organizations, much of what you read here may either be supported by or hindered by upper management and/or company leadership. There are many ways to both strategically and, in some cases, cost effectively impact quality, improve service, and continuously improve in general. If these strategic goals are launched from above the manager they are most likely championed by leadership, supported, and should trickle down to managers, supervisors, and staff. However, if these strategic goals are initiated by the manager, without support of leadership it may be tantamount to shouting into the wind or the single ant attempting to push the pebble by himself. This can be very frustrating to the manager who has gained useful insight and understands the methods and their benefits but is powerless to enact them.

Over the years I have witnessed much regarding what works well and what does not in and around the IT service Management arena, and unfortunately, a good many of the failures that I have witnessed were directly related to managers themselves or leadership. This is often attributable to the lack of effective communications and coordination between the two, for various reasons. Missing in their communications can be clear instructions or definitions for current goals in one direction, and information concerning risks and issues that exist within operations, with staff, of regarding clients in the other. Another primary issue tends to be that there are times when the more strategic, client aligned, or business supportive initiatives are overlooked in lieu of actions that are perceived by company leadership as more directly beneficial to the 'bottom-line' (actions that more immediately reflect positively in the accounting books and P&L statements). When times are hard, these actions may include reducing staff (thus removing their salaries from the expense ledger) and often this action may involve letting go the most tenured and experienced staff due to their salary rate. A company may also resort to reducing benefits and incentives, hiring less expensive (and thus less experienced) technical resources, and perform other actions designed to reflect a better profit margin today.

This is not a strategy that works over time. The internal issues will still exist and ultimately, due to the lack of timely attention to these core problems, the company's supporting architecture becomes weak. Attempting to build upon this dilapidated infrastructure worsens the issue and the company may continue to falter. In other words, cutting quality costs (investments made to achieve and maintain quality) and removing valuable personnel may initially make the company look more profitable but ultimately will impact service delivery, upset client's, and impact revenue, which in turn creates a need to start the negative cycle all over again. I refer to this as an **'uncontrolled cascade cycle of failure'**.

This also tends to create a fearful and uncertain environment amongst the technical staff (usually engineers and administrators) who will not become engaged, will not or cannot perform at their peak, and the best of them may seek employment elsewhere in an attempt to stabilize their lives. This additional loss of knowledge, familiarity with infrastructure and procedures, and relationships with clients will in turn impact service delivery as well as client confidence. Ultimately, the immediate profit focused shortsightedness may have a deleterious impact on the 3 areas that effect long-term company success and business stability the most – the client, the staff, and the culture - and thus, the cycle continues.

The main but simple point that sometimes seems to be missed is that all things within a company are connected (in the way that all of the gears in a clock are connected), vital to its operation, and impact the desired outcome: the delivery of accurate time – which directly relates to the perception of value to the person who has invested in the clock.

There is an inherent synergy between leadership, staff and staff performance, management astuteness and ability, company-wide focus on client satisfaction, sales, project management, and other constituent parts of a company. Companies also sometimes fail to realize that championing improvement, quality, and satisfaction leads to retention at all levels - (not only retention of customers and employees, but also of revenue, stability, and reputation). If you doubt this, just take a look behind the scenes of some of the most successful business today – they get it.

Possible solution: As opposed to cutting personnel, quality costs, incentives, and improvement initiatives, an alternate more insightful and ecumenical means for exacting positive change and improving the bottom line would be to examine performance costs associated with poor quality, waste, and efficiencies with regards to day-to-day operations. It helps to periodically audit policies, processes, and procedures to reduce or remove the costs associated with poor quality (mentioned more in chapter 1, these costs are removed directly from revenue). This in turn can increases capacity, ability, and availability of resources and allows the current staff to do more for the client with less effort and with less waste. This can lead to increased client satisfaction and in addition reduces stress on the current staff (thus increasing retention and performance). Your efforts could include examining variances within service delivery as well as across staff and within process execution (variances within process efficiencies) and determining where effort is being spent that does not produce anything beneficial to client or company. Examining KPIs and other metrics will help with your understanding of how to produce better quality from existing staff at less cost. This is what I refer to as '**Lean Operational Strategy**' – doing more with less, doing it more efficiently and effectively, and providing more capacity at less cost.

Contrary to the previous example (where valuable elements may be discarded by the company), these actions help to engage, empower, and reduce stress on staff while at the same time enhances overall performance and increases client satisfaction. These actions also allow for additional client demand to be managed by the same number of staff due to the reduction of wasted time, effort, and attention. The retention of staff also lends to knowledge retention and consistently presents the same faces to the clients over time, which increases client confidence. As a result, you have created a cycle that is the opposite of the previously mentioned negative cycle.

Everyone within leadership, from CEO down to supervisor, needs to take responsibility for the quality that sits within their area of care, control, and obligation. If this starts at the top, it creates a shell within a shell, within a shell of quality. In order for a well informed and professional manager to take root and become effective, leadership needs to become an advocate of quality and work with management to ensure quality with people, processes, performance, and culture. In this scenario, a company's quality system is championed from above – it becomes embedded within their mission and core values.

My personal definition of quality

I see quality as <u>the attention to detail, resiliency, and other key client focused considerations regarding the final design parameters of a product or service and the dedication of effort to achieving those parameters.</u>

In short: quality takes focus on design and dedication to excellence to achieve.

Leaders must set the tone. They need to always be strategic, professional, honorable, compassionate, ethical, and well aware of the best methodologies, tools, insights, and industry standards related to their business, and their long-term goals. This is how you garner loyalty, retain staff, build positive relationships, and effectively set the stage for quality and continuous improvement within the company and value for the clients you serve.

Moral leadership inspires ethical behavior. Insightful leadership creates a solid direction, honorable leadership assures that the proper paths are chosen, and a win/win/win cycle can be created between company, staff, and client. This 3-way win cycle is what I call the '**circle of business synergy**': good employees deliver good service to the customers, who in turn are happy with the service and generate revenue for the company, who in turn can provide better security and compensation to the employees, and on and on – this is a win/win/win scenario that works!

Kaizen
Levin j. Allen – 2017

Levin J. Allen

CHAPTER 1

The IT Manager

Focus on Managers

From what I have experienced, issues can and do occur when hiring managers or directors fail to realize the critical role that the IT manager plays regarding various aspects of day-to-day operations and overall business performance. The IT manager is in fact a critical lynchpin between upper management, clients, and staff. It is critical to your company that leadership, upper management as well as middle managers understand that the person in this roll needs to have the experience, maturity, and professional acumen to provide a functional balance across all three areas to insure both efficient and effective operations overall. Selecting the right person for this roll is critical to all areas of service operations as well as day to day business continuity. An effective manager can assist your company a great deal regarding client satisfaction, staff retention, and planning across parallel and interdependent departments, such as Sales, Project Management (PMO), Finance, and Human Resources (HR). The combined and synergistic relationships between all of these, as well as other, departments help to assure business continuity and smoother operations from day to day.

Of all the reasons people leave companies, having a bad manager tops the list. According to Gallup polls, a full 50% of employees who quit cite their manager as the reason. - (Voices, V. 2017)

An effective Manager:

- Must be fair, impartial, and empathetic – a person in this role attempting to manage too strong equates to being a "hatchet man", too weak and he can be ignored and ineffectual. He or she must provide sound guidance and direction as well as set the example of what the IT department and company expectations for general attitude and culture should be

- Must know how to manage his or herself (emotions, attitude, and professionalism). He or she should have a firm understanding of who he/she is as well as his/her strengths and weaknesses. This allows them to address unexpected staff or operational issues without being caught off-guard and to make quicker and sounder decisions. This awareness can evoke a sense of confidence and sure-footedness.

- Should be able to maintain situational awareness regarding all key areas and components under his/her care and control. This allows him/her to understand how current status, events, and information will impact day-to-day operations. This also helps to prevent unknown variables from suddenly impacting operations (due to poor planning or vetting) – events that could take considerable time, resource, or costs to rectify. (See "Managing Quality Costs later in this chapter")

Everything that occurs is based on this simple premise:
"It would not have happened, had it not been for..."
(L. Allen 2020)

I submit that for everything that occurs, there had have been a series of steps, events, and/or decisions that led up to the occurrence - either good or bad. This is about causality (cause and effect). This can either be related to "think ahead, plan ahead, to be ahead" or "hindsight is a bear". Business can be compared to the game of Chess where strategy, foresight, planning, and in a lot of cases statistical analysis. Also see 'Root cause analysis'

Just a few monumental disasters of the past predicated on either hubris, or poorly vetted planning:

- o   Boeing MCAS and the 737 MAX

- o   Fukushima Daiichi nuclear disaster

- o   Word trade center disaster

- o   The Nedelin catastrophe

- o   The Titanic syncing

- o   The Apollo 1 near catastrophe

- o   Chernobyl

- Must provide leadership and structure to his/her team as well as adhere, and if possible, lend to the strategic direction, quality goals, and principles of the company

- Must focus on Maintaining a balanced score card (between Client/Staff/Stakeholders) as well as between Financial performance, process performance, and client satisfaction. He/she must lead by example, set the tone, and be the role model that leads the department's culture in the most positive and constructive direction

- Must be passionate about data — data lends to information, metrics, and KPIs which in turn lends to accurate awareness and sound strategic planning. The more information you have, the more informed decisions you are able to make

The manager's impact on and responsibility to culture

An organization's culture is the everyday manifestation of its underlying values and traditions. It shows up in how employees behave at work, what their expectations are of the organization and each other, and what is considered normal in terms of how employees approach their jobs. (Pyzdek & Keller, 2010)

I have had the opportunity to work for a few companies where the culture was what, quite frankly, could have been considered as extremely bad - I say opportunity because it gave me a chance to experience first-hand the impact (emotions, feelings, frustrations, and real-life effect on staff performance) when attempting to effectively operate in such environments. In looking back, I would site some of the reasons for the cultural difficulties as being due to either dictatorial leadership, disconnected upper management, leadership whose focus was blindly fixated on profits as opposed to quality, or a closed ear to staff complaints, suggestions, or recommendations by upper management. In addition, I will add the disheartening lack of empathy to the clients to whom services were sold. In a couple cases there was an acute lack of understanding by leadership of how to manage their business culture and the impact that this had on day-to-day operations - this encompassed the treatment of staff.

"Less than one-third of Americans are engaged in their jobs in any given year. This finding has remained consistent since 2000, when Gallup first began measuring and reporting on U.S. workplace engagement. Gallup defines engaged employees as those who are involved in, enthusiastic about and committed to their work and workplace." - (Gallup, 2015)

Lastly, with regards to this specific topic, I have purposefully avoided adding any links to this manuscript as I am aware that there can be cases where the server, domain, or site that the link directs the reader can change over time, which can be problematic if the link is embedded within a document. However, I will make an exception in this case only because how specifically poignant the subject matter is and the specific relevance to this topic.

The subject matter is a short documentary from all the way back in 1937 called 'The Boss Didn't Say Good Morning' put out by MGM. Within the space of 10 minutes this short movie succinctly conveys how a boss's approach, attention to, or even awareness of how his actions can impact not only the mindset and mood of his employees, but how it can reach all the way to impacting the employee's family life as well. If this link should not be available any time after this book is published, I encourage you to Google the title to see if you are able to locate it on the web. The link points to the DailyMotion web site and the content illustrates that even as far back as the 1930s it was understood that the impact on staff engagement, peace of mind, and even home-life can be impacted by what occurs in the office:
http://www.dailymotion.com/video/x1z4ex3

I highly recommend any manager or direct boss review this short film and determine its value and if it changes their perspective on how they relate to their staff.

Gauge and understand the quality of self

One of the things that a good manager needs to manage is himself - first and foremost, both his/her emotions and his/her professionalism. This ability tends to be coupled with maturity and usually comes about naturally over time with a combination of experience (both successes and failures) and an individual's character, training, personal growth and development, interactions, and natural inclination towards leadership and self-control.

A manager's self-confidence is derived from his/her successes, achievements, and the self-awareness of his/her capabilities. His/her fears tend to be derived from past failures and the self-awareness of his/her deficiencies. There are also considerations for one's natural ability to be honest, focused, honorable, empathetic, courageous (when it comes to doing the right things even when difficult), diplomatic, and decisive. This holds true for anyone in a leadership position.

He/she must realize who "their", as an individual, customers are (internal, external, and holistically). As a manager, my customers are my clients as well as my staff, upper management, and business leadership. This could also include any vendors or others connected to the business that I come into contact with on a regular basis. I purposely interact with all these groups as if they were my direct customers by way of open, honest, and clear communications, promoting synergy, and doing my best to continuously anticipate their respective needs, issues, and concerns.

helpful insight:

Starting that new position

A good new manager –

1. Needs to be strong enough to not be broken down and rendered ineffective by his new and possibly unstructured environment –
2. Needs to be strong enough to push back and place things on their proper path, to lead by example, and to be an effective change agent for his company –
3. Needs to be astute and focused enough to analyze his environment and gain situational awareness quickly –
4. Needs to be wise enough to judiciously communicate effectively both up to his superiors as well as down to his subordinates –
5. Needs to be diplomatic enough to effectively deal with issues related to staff, client, or operations that fall under his purview

Over time, as an IT manager and across several positions, I have developed a personal on-boarding methodology which allows me to bring myself up to speed and achieve a degree of operational efficiency within a relatively short period of time. My methodology is comprised of 6 main tasks:

   1.   Gain situational awareness as soon as possible (how can you be responsible if you are not situationally aware?). This awareness focus includes current issues, successes, about the staff as individuals and as a group, processes and procedures, policies, assets, infrastructure, and anything additional that is specific to the position's performance at the time. From there it is vital to maintain awareness over time as it is a dynamic discernment at best.

   2.   Build team dynamics (trust, communications, connections, synergy, and action) – Building trust with your team is vital to open communications and day-to-day

operational efficiency. It also lends to building a culture that is positive, minimizes staff stress, and in return can reduce staff churn rate. It is also important to be fair, personable, and empathetic along with business minded, vigilant, and motivating. When I mention vigilant, it means to know what an individual's past and current performance levels are as well as any, needs, perspectives, or issues that they may need assist with or of any course corrections that may be needed before problems arise. One of an effective manager's greatest advantages is foreknowledge.

3.   Making sure I understand my role and authorities – (how can you be held accountable if you do not know what you are accountable for?). This is vital in order to avoid overstepping your authority and this lends clarity regarding what you can and should be doing, managing, initiating, tracking, collecting, analyzing, and addressing within the confines of your roll or position. You should also know what level of flexibility you have regarding managing your staff - everything from rewarding or promoting to reprimanding and termination.

4.   Examine current process effectiveness and efficiency – Knowing if processes are effective, are being periodically reviewed and updated over time, are known by all, and are readily available for reference by all who need to adhere to them is vital. A good parallel of why this is important can be drawn from the works of Sun Tzu in 'the Art of War' where he states that "If instructions are not clear and commands not explicit, it is the commander's fault. But if the orders are clear it is the fault of the subordinate that the instructions are not followed." This being said, it is vital that policies, processes, and procedures are reviewed and updated on a regular basis to assure that they are both relevant and timely - these are the instructions that all are to follow and should be clear.

Policies, Processes, and procedures, these documents serve as the "Guide-rails" that are established and put in place to keep everyone on the proper paths and to mitigate the risk of someone going astray and negatively impacting service or operations. In addition, they should be posted in a location that is readily accessible by all who need to know and follow them - if they are not available for review by those who are to be held accountable but may not be sure, how can they be accurately followed?

5.   Determine key KPIs – this is an essential step that lends to situational awareness as it allows you to focus on the information that reveals the most about critical areas of concern both dynamically and over time. Selecting and monitoring Key Performance Indicators is a fairly straightforward means of tracking and evaluating data and information that is critical to your understanding how well your department is performing relative to your contractual SLAs. A few KPIs that are traditionally germane to Service Management are:

- Staff performance metrics
- Service performance metrics
- Support response time
- SLA adherence percentages
- Service backlog statistics
- Resource capacity utilization
- Solution Retouch / First Pass Quality statistics
- Client satisfaction feedback and ratings
- Staff Retention/Churn rate
- Average Staff Tenure
- Time to hire
- Absenteeism metrics

KPIs can be grouped together under categories such as performance KPIs, staff KPIs, client KPIs and so on – this makes it easier to set up dashboards.

The metrics tracked and KPIs monitored may differ from company to company - depending on what your specific obligations and strategic goals are. The KPIs mentioned above are just a sample of metrics related to Service management, support, and delivery. It is also important to note that what you track is critical to the value of the information compiled from the metrics and your ability to make effective change based on the information. Note that viewing metrics during the course of the day provides a static snapshot of where things may currently sit that day; however, viewing metrics over time provides a perspective of change over time and trending - this is where the most insightful perspectives can be drawn and where solid analysis can be made.

6. Effectively communicate both upstream and downstream – this is another area that lends to maintaining situational awareness. This is also a critical piece regarding business continuity and mitigates the risk of issues occurring due to someone not being aware or informed.

Another on-boarding exercises that I traditionally undergo is early checking of the staff's situational awareness regarding safety and security. I do this because I came to realize at some point that often your new staff may not actually be aware of security protocols, where the fire extinguishers and alarm boxes are located, what the emergency evacuation plans are, protocols for communicating during disasters, etc. This may not seem to be too big an issue up front; however, as they say - hindsight is a bear.

Failure to provide and make sure that your team is aware of security protocols can be very detrimental to the company's well-being from the perspectives of liability, personal safety, and company security. For example, would all your staff know how to respond if they notice a stranger roaming the offices unattended? There have been cases where this has occurred and not one person challenged the person's presence or approached them to find out what they were there for or to offer assist. A simple "Hello, may I help you?" would let someone who was there with nefarious intentions (hurt someone, steal something, or even spying) know that they have been spotted. It would also offer genuine assist to someone who was lost or searching for someone specific.

Bringing your team up to speed regarding security and safety awareness is not only important, but also a legal requirement. According to the US Department of Labor, Occupational Safety and Health Administration (OSHA), among many other requirements, a company must:

Establish or update operating procedures and communicate them so that employees follow safety and health requirements.
Employers must provide safety training in a language and vocabulary workers can understand. (OSHA, 2018)

3 Primary Management Goals:

1. To help assure that the company is successful by accurately and effectively transmitting and proliferating its mission, vision, and strategic goals while building good client relationships, and creating solid paths for solid revenue streams and business continuity. (looking out for the company)

2.   To help assure that your team is successful by providing good leadership, guidance, and support and making sure that they have the tools and training to be effective at what they do (looking out for the staff)

3.   To listen to customer insights, opinions, and pain points in order to make sure that their service delivery or their support is not inadvertently negatively impacted due to lack of managerial attention or awareness (looking out for the client)

Balanced Score Cards

Within Six Sigma, paying equal attention to client, staff, and company owners/leadership is considered maintaining a "Balanced Score-card". It is important to attempt to maintain a balanced focus across all 3 major areas of responsibility. Maintaining this focus allows for awareness and management of both performance and issues that may arise in any of the three areas and helps with addressing issues before they become larger problems as they travel away from their point of inception. Focusing too much on one area can allow you to lose sight of the other two allowing performance lapses to occur.

Another set of 3 focus points that need to remain balanced are client satisfaction, financial performance, and the effectiveness and efficacy of processes and procedures; once again, if you focus too much on one area you can cause detriment to the others.

Managing Quality Costs

During my time as an IT manager one of the biggest contributors to the costs associated with poor quality has been retouch. These are times when during a support call or service request an engineer attempted, but failed, to resolve an issue to the client's satisfaction (or deliver a solution that meets the parameters or quality of an agreement). This creates a need to revisit the issue (on the same day, a different day, or even worse across several days) - spending more time and effort, off the clock, to correct the issue. This time is then no longer available for other billable service work that could have been occurring during the time. This issue can also be impacted further when the original attending engineer is not available to follow up to correct the issue and an alternate resource needs to be used. The problem with this is that the initial engineer has a sense of what he or she has performed or changed to reach the current state, whereas the alternate resource may not. This lack of familiarity or historical reference (if not captured in service logs or other means of knowledge transfer) can actually lead to a prolonged solution and making the issue worse. This failure also upsets the client and can lead to loss of their confidence or even canceled or not renewed contracts.

Note that this is just one form of quality cost - there are many others that tend to hide just below the surface of a company's purview that may not be so obvious, yet cumulatively have significant impact on a company's bottom line. In addition, quality costs can be either positive - costs beneficial to maintaining quality in the form of an investment in time, effort, or resource or it can be negative - detrimental to quality due to improper vetting, poor management or oversight, or waste. One of the most succinct descriptions of what quality costs are that I have come across was in the Six Sigma Handbook during my training:

Quality costs are the total of the costs incurred by:

a) Investing in the prevention of non-conformances to requirements (investment cost);

b) Appraising a product or service for conformance to requirements (investment cost)

c) Failure to meet requirements (cost of poor quality) - This includes retouch, re-work, or wasted time, motion, resource, or effort. (Pyzdek & Keller, 2010)

Essentially, a company needs to invest in the creation of quality to assure quality in its products and services.

It is also important to mention that the cost of poor quality related to a specific event can grow as the event moves further along the line from the initial oversight and moves towards the client's view or experience. For example, if a software engineer is working on a client's web site and mistakenly adds an erroneous character to one of the URL links within a page but it is noticed by the manager, supervisor, or someone within the company before the page goes live - the costs in time and impact are minimal for the engineer to revisit the code and fix the problem. However, if the mistake makes it all the way to the client's site and the client (or one of their customers) notices, then the cost and impact related to fixing the issue will be greater. There may also be inconvenience or possible business impact to the client, and you will now have a client who has lost confidence in your ability to provide the value that they expected. This incident, or even worst multiple events during the course of the year, may come into consideration when it comes time to renew contracts. There may also be fines related to Service Level Agreements (SLAs) that are not met. These costs may be extracted directly from what would have been revenue.

The second most prominent cause of poor-quality costs that I have encountered has been staff churn rate. This is due to several factors combined that cumulatively can costs a company a great deal in time, effort, and money, as well as stability and client good will. The primary factors involved are:

The loss of investment - when hiring a new employee, a company may invest a good deal of time, effort, and expense advertising for the position, sorting through resumes, scheduling, and holding interviews, performing background checks and other HR and on-boarding activities. They will then need to make the necessary infrastructure changes (to accommodate accounts, phone extensions, computer equipment, business cards, etc.). There is also time spent on training to bring the new hire up to speed so that he or she is familiar with the processes, systems, equipment, accounts, and more. This investment can sometimes be considerable; however, if that employee chooses or is asked to leave in a few months the investment becomes waste, and the process needs to be initiated all over again.

"Studies on the cost of employee turnover are all over the board.
Some studies (such as SHRM) predict that every time a business replaces a salaried employee, it costs 6 to 9 months' salary on average. For a manager making $40,000 a year, that is $20,000 to $30,000 in recruiting and training expenses.
But others predict the cost is even more--that losing a salaried employee can cost as much as twice their annual salary, especially for a high-earner or executive-level employee." (Merhar, 2018)

The loss of knowledge - There are times, especially within IT service and support, where you may have a couple of high-end, deeply knowledgeable engineers who have been around for years and know the client's infrastructure and how it was constructed like the back of their hand. They may also be on a comfortable first name basis with their respective clients. In one sense, this is a good thing; however, in another it can be very precarious - especially if that person chooses to leave the company, has not documented half of the critical information that they hold in their head, and there is no chance for adequate knowledge transfer prior to his/her leaving.

The loss of continuity - After some point, when a company's operations have been consistent for a while service and support capacity levels out - there tends to be adequate resources to manage the average daily service loads to the satisfaction of the client - in some cases, just barely – a state of equilibrium with capacity management.

(Capacity management is primarily based on three factors: resource efficiency, resource availability, and demand).

If a resource leaves abruptly the delicate balance of resource ability and availability to demand can be disrupted. This can cause 2 events that have a very negative impact on quality to occur overnight: (1) the workload needs to be taken up by all other resources in order to maintain the current service levels - this has the potential of both stressing the remaining resources and impacts the quality of service rendered to the client, which leads to (2) the client becomes upset due the diminished quality of service and the change is impacting their day-to-day operations. Note, this condition can remain until a new position is advertised, applicants are interviewed, and a candidate is hired, on-boarded, and brought up to speed. (See the section in chapter 3 regarding capacity management and efficiency).

The loss of client confidence - It may be a bit naive to think that your clients do not notice when the engineers attending to their service and support needs change over time. This is especially true if they usually interact with their engineers for assigned service request or support efforts. It would also be reasonable to believe that at some time there will be a point, due to constant employee churn, where your client's concern peaks and their confidence in your ability to manage your own company, let alone their contracted needs, comes into consideration.

When these things occur on a regular basis (and I have seen this with a few companies first-hand), then the costs are detrimental to revenue and bottom-line accounting - after substantially impacting both staff and client along the way. This is traditionally where service begins to slip more, the clients become disgruntled, revenue is impacted further, and the negative downward spiral start.

According to an article recently written in the Huffington Post: "Unhappy employees cost companies worldwide billions of dollars per year in lost revenues, settlements and various other damages. The loss of revenue can send well-known companies into financial distress, with some filing for bankruptcy. Employee negligence due to dissatisfaction with their employer leads to much of the financial losses suffered by major brands and companies of all sizes." (Agrawal, 2016)

You can find similar insights and reporting across all the major business news sites that periodically report on this and other business and organizational concerns; sites such as Forrester.com, Gartner.com, Forbes.com, US News, Bloomberg.com, CNN, entrepreneur.com, and others. In fact, because there are so many articles written to address this topic, it should be apparent that this is a genuine issue for companies and organizations and that it should be high on the list of issues that a company's leadership has targeted to be addressed.

Additionally, as mentioned above, staff retention, or conversely staff churn rate, should be one of the main KPIs focused on by any company whose staff are integral to client service or support. There seems to be a critical, inherent, symbiotic relationship between staff and company that is sometimes missed entirely, and it is based on the premise of mutually balanced expectations, long-term stability and growth, day-to-day satisfaction, and value (much the same as the relationship between a company and its client or husband and wife).

Standardization

Another important consideration for fluid operations is standardization of both hardware and software. A few of the benefits for standardization are:

- 'Big Buy' price breaks from vendors – often hardware and software vendors will offer huge price breaks per unit or license in return for large volume purchases. This is a win / win scenario as it works for you with regards to maintaining standardization and reduced cost and for the vendor due to the bulk sales

- Ease of maintenance and support for the service staff – with this regard, day to day operations becomes a lot easier for your service staff when they only have 1 or 2 standard desktop or laptop models or applications brands to support. In addition, operations costs related to certifications and training are reduced due to the need to focus on fewer vendors, makes, models, and packages

- Less cost and diversity with regards to training of staff across the organization – with both new and existing staff, in-house training and familiarization with the company's hardware and software complement becomes less hectic when dealing with a standard make/model/form factor/package

- Better support via the ability to swap out a faulty hardware component or device with a standard form factor component – user downtime can be reduced if support issues can be resolved by simply swapping out the computer, hard drive, monitor, or printer with a standard inventory item and working on servicing the faulty part off-line

- The ability to plan ahead with your vendors regarding technology pre-testing and model replacement vetting – In the past I have worked closely with several big brand name vendors, such as HP, Dell, and Lenovo and often due to the volume purchasing related to standardized form factors they will share their product road map with you to coordinate the next available models to be released in their product line. Usually, a non-disclosure agreement would need to be signed. Also, in most cases they can allow the early release of an evaluation unit to you so that you can evaluate staging, imaging, and compatibility prior to the actual release date of the model. This helps greatly with avoiding technology "Black Holes" within your IT department or being forced to switch to a different manufacture at the last minute causing an unplanned mixed technology within your infrastructure.

One highly effective way that I have been able to manage standards in the past is by building and maintaining vetted and enforced Approved Product Lists (APLs) and Approved Software Lists (ASLs). This is especially useful when there are several departments within the company who have their own budgets for hardware and software procurement. This prevents rogue or difficult to support or maintain elements from inadvertently entering inventory and causing compatibility, support, or other issues downstream.

On Meetings

Meetings are an essential part of everyday business. They serve as an arena for several individuals or groups to come together to share ideas, work out strategies, review progress or change, or any number of other collaborative topics. Below are a few brief notes on areas of focus with regards to meetings based on my experiences.

Coordinate meeting times - just because a proposed meeting time is good for some does not mean it works for all other's schedules. This becomes more critical as the topic of the meeting becomes important. Often a company uses shared calendars within their infrastructure build-out, an example of this would be Microsoft Outlook. This program allows you to better plan for meetings and completeness of attendance by checking for available time slots across all invitees. Locating common availability time for all the people to be invited as well as the availability of the conference room itself greatly reduces the chances for under-attendance or arriving at the designated meeting location just to find that it is currently occupied. It is also a good idea to check for meeting acceptances, rejections, or tentative responses from the invited attendees - this may give you a good indication in advance if the meeting may need to be rescheduled or if the attendance is tracking well.

Notes should be taken in meetings to capture topic related action items, follow up items, and good ideas - once again, this becomes more critical as the topic of the meeting becomes important. I have attended many meetings where many great ideas for projects, planning, next steps, and strategy were discussed but were lost in time because they were never documented nor followed up on after the meeting ended. These ideas often resurface during subsequent meetings, which constitutes a waste of time and progress as the results of the follow up items from the first meeting could have been input to the second meeting - allowing for actual progress.

Action or follow up items should be assigned an owner and an estimated time for completion should be recorded. It is a good idea with consecutive meetings to use the notes or minutes from the previous meeting as part of the agenda of the current meeting - this way all progress and information is captures and items that still require attention can be reassigned and placed in motion for the next meeting.

Helpful Insight:

Meetings
- All who are required to attend, should - care should be taken by the organizer to assure optimal attendance and the meeting location is booked

- All should attend on time - needing to delay the start of a meeting because there are individuals who have not arrived on time is wasteful. The same holds true for meetings that start on time and great ideas are discussed but missed by those showing up late - their possible valuable insights and feedback is then missed

- Minutes or notes should be taken, especially when they may be needed for follow up or meeting reviews - this is critical to maintaining progress and "getting as much mileage" as possible from each meeting, optimizing time and effort, and reducing waste

o Confidentiality level should be set - if the topic of discussion is confidential, for attendee's ears only, or business critical and should not be conveyed nor made available outside of the confines of the meeting, then this should be made clear at the beginning and at the end of the meeting

o Focus on the objective topic, sans any distractions or "rabbits" - This is a very important consideration regarding wasted meeting time, and I have seen it occur during quite a few meetings. It occurs when someone brings up a topic that is not germane to the intended topic of the meeting (a rabbit), engages someone else with regards to this topic and the conversation cascades off track. I have seen this eat up to 30 percent of the intended meeting's topic time while adding no intrinsic value to the meeting whatsoever. In meetings words take time, wasted words equals wasted time - It is advantageous focus on what is most essential and productive. I usually mention at the beginning of important meetings that it is especially important to remain focused on the topic during the meeting time.

Helpful Information and Recommendations

The below information is offered primarily via my experiences and partially by way of general observations, conversations with other managers, and research on related concepts and events. There are many, many more insightful and informative resources available; however, my intention is to share that which I have found useful during my trek through IT business management over the years.

Things that can possibly slow you down:

- The lack of professional conduct within management (other / parallel managers)

- Half answers (due to people not really knowing and being too busy or not caring enough to find out)

- Applications freezing or computer malfunctions

- You do not have or cannot receive needed tools

- Insufficient coordination with other team leaders

- The lack of collaboration with other departments (with regards to parallel or competing initiatives)

- The lack of effective communication in general (culture issue)

- Cross talk and tomfoolery during meetings

- The lack of fundamental policies, process, and procedural documentation

- Old and no longer accurate documentation

- Deficient or not well vetted staff on-boarding processes

- The loss of valuable and needed resources due to disconnected and not collaborated upper management decisions

- Loss of knowledge, experience, and valuable, embedded resource if the above bulleted item occurs

- Lack of traction on planned well vetted initiatives due to competing needs

- The lack of standardization

A Word on Planning

Major types of planning to consider:

Operational - daily/weekly

Tactical – yearly or less

Strategic - long term, 5 year

Contingency – "what if..." planning - even the best business planners can neglect this consideration during operations planning. I have seen business suffer greatly due to lack of contingency, continuity, or disaster recovery (DR) planning

Logistical - (what are the most critical issues and what are the most available and fruitful opportunities) this envelopes all the other planning considerations and serves as a launch-point for any operational brainstorming and planning

Planning is critical and integral to sustained improvement - To survive we need to stand in the present while examining the past, learning, and appropriately planning for the future.

To survive well we need to learn from our mistakes and always improve our next steps – avoiding repeating our mistakes. This way we assure that we are consistently planning to do better tomorrow then we did today.

In addition, I will mention under the topic of planning that it is critical for both Demand Management and Capacity Management that you continuously assess your ability to support the services you sell prior to selling them. This will assure that you never break your staff nor disappoint your customers - continually assess your capabilities as this is a dynamic and ever-changing consideration. (See Capacity management in chapter 3)

Recommendations:

For the following recommendations I am adding just a brief definition or explanation for each - my goal is to make you aware of the existence of each theory or model and provide a sense of their potential value-add to you or your company. Beyond that, I recommend that if you desire a deeper understanding of a specific concept or feel that any may be relevant to your operations or strategic goals and objectives that you research it on-line. This further investigation will allow you to become more familiar with the underlying specifics related to each term and thus gain an extremely broad and wide-ranging conceptualization and understanding of it.

What every manager should know or at least be familiar with:

- **The vital importance of the VOC** - This is a fairly important acronym for any company that provides either goods or services to a paying client and depends on the satisfaction of that client to maintain revenue streams and remain profitable in business. It stands for 'Voice of the Customer' and represents just that. The voice of the customer identifies the customer's needs and expectations of your company's products or services. It is how well your company meets these expectations that provides a measure of value to the consumer. It is up to the company's leadership to listen to this voice and determine what product or service attributes will provide the value that (a) brings the customer to them to fill their initial needs, (b) keeps the customer satisfied enough to keep them paying for the product or service from your company continually over time (customer loyalty), and (c) prevents the customer from deciding to spend somewhere else, where they may perceive the value to be greater (beating the competition). I will add a quick note that "Value" as perceived by the customer may be measured via the quality of the product or service as well as the astuteness of its support and/or its relative cost, amongst other variables.

- **The Kano Model** - This model was developed by Noriyaki Kano and consists of a graph (set of axis where 3 types of requirements can be plotted and assessed) and its associated methodology that aligns the proficiency of requirement fulfillment with customer satisfaction. The graph's grid has a horizontal access that depicts how well a requirement was met and a vertical access the shows the degree of client satisfaction. It allows you to better understand how 3 key customer requirements (basic quality, performance, and delight) contribute to or detract from their satisfaction.

- **Parkinson's Law** - This law, named after C. N. Parkinson (1909–93) the British historian and writer who formulated it, the law states that "Work expands so as to fill the time available for its completion". It was derived from a study of how bureaucracies can grow over time despite the need for their resources diminishing (such as how the British Admiralty grew from year to year from 1914 to 1928 while the number of ships and the size of the navy decreased over those same years) and subsequently how people tend to leverage all the time allotted to perform work over early completion and optimization over time. Regarding this phenomenon, I have seen this at times when my daughter would bring home a homework assignment that was due in a week; however, I would find her hard at work on it the night before it was due. Understanding this law will help you with time management by helping you to assign realistic time intervals in which to complete routine daily tasks for yourself and your staff.

- **The Pareto Principle** - This principle is also known as the 80/20 rule, the law of the vital few, and the principle of factor sparsity. It fundamentally states that for many events, roughly 80% of the effects come from 20% of the causes. Examples of this in everyday life could be how 20 percent of professional golfers take home 80 percent of the prizes, or how 20 percent of church goers are responsible for 80 percent of the offerings. In IT support this can equate to how 80 percent of the technical issues stem from 20 percent of the problems. Root cause analysis can be used in most cases to associate various issues to a specific problem - in these cases if you identify and solve the core problem the various issues that arise from it are resolved as well.

- **The Yerkes–Dodson law** - This law asserts that a certain amount of anxiety can enhance performance; however, this is only up to a point where anxiety reaches the upper limit of the curve and then anxiety starts to decrease performance. I have seen this occur in cases where engineers are overtaxed, having too much to do in too little time and performance drops with regards to all the initiatives being worked on. I used to have a saying for this - If you try to get 10 pounds of potatoes into a 5-pound bag, one of 3 things will happen: (1) you'll end up with a bag of half potatoes, (2) you'll end up with a bag containing only half of the potatoes, or (3) the bag will break. When affixing this analogy to human resources, the first two can greatly impact service, the third can devastate a resource - I have seen it happen - literally. This is a somewhat obscure law; however, I see it as vital when it comes to understanding and managing stress and stress related failures within your departments.

- **The Dunning-Kruger Effect** - In the field of psychology, the Dunning–Kruger effect is a cognitive bias of illusory superiority - the inability of people to recognize their lack of ability. It can be interpreted as the lack of capability or awareness of people with a low ability to effectively manage a task, to realize it; and can result in the case where they will overestimate their ability – to both themselves and to others. They are not able to accurately assess the proficiency of their own skills – or lack thereof.

- **Sun Tzu – Quote on clear instruction to troops** - this is one of my favorite quotes from 'The Art of War' and I often keep a framed copy of it above my desk. The quote goes: "If instructions are not clear and commands not explicit, it is the commander's fault. But if the orders are clear it is the fault of the subordinate that the instructions are not followed." - This points out an extremely critical connection between clear and consistent instructions (policies, processes, or procedures) not being followed, and responsibility. Every time that you ask someone to perform a task, try to ask yourself if your instructions are clear and explicit.

- **The difference between Moral and Ethical** - I have found that often these two terms are simply not understood or juxtaposed. Basically, Moral reflects your personal conscience and principals, your knowing what is right from wrong (a moral man knows that it is wrong to rob a bank). Ethical is related to behavior and is usually governed by laws, taboos, and codes of conduct - which, if they are violated, go against established protocol (an ethical man would not rob a bank because it is wrong). To remember which relates to what, just think of having a 'Moral Compass' and your 'Ethical Behavior'. Example: Even though it was morally wrong, it was unethical of the doctor to remove the patient's gall bladder for no reason and without consent. In the arena of service management, it is always best to be a person with good morals, conduct yourself ethically, and to have staff and leadership that are the same.

- **The Meaning of Kaizen** - Kaizen is a Continuous Improvement Process. It is an ongoing effort to improve products, services, people, support, productivity, or processes at all levels at all times - and is ongoing, forever. The efforts can be realized in the form of smaller "incremental" improvements over time (such as better ways to perform minor or daily tasks) or via a large, focused improvement (such as a project). Process efficiencies are continuously evaluated and improved regardless of their current level of effectiveness and anyone from lowest to highest position within a company can contribute.

  - **ITIL's CSI 7 Step Improvement Process** - Within the 5th book of ITIL 'Continuous Improvement' (the first four books are specific to Service Strategy, Service Design, Service Transition, and Service Operation) there is listed 7 steps that can be used as a process for continuous improvement. These steps allow you to work more efficiently, reduce waste and other costs of poor quality, and allows for growth and innovation that can keep you one step ahead of your competition. The 7 steps are:
    1. Identify the approach for improvement
    2. State what will you measure

3. Collect the Data
4. Process the data
5. Analyze the data and information
6. Present and use the information
7. Implement corrective or remedial activities

In addition, the Four P's of ITIL Service Delivery stand for:

1. People: People are in charge of providing IT services. These professionals should have the skills and competencies required for providing services

2. Products: The products are the tools, services, and technology used in the delivery of, and support of, the services

3. Processes: Processes support and manage the services being offered so that the services meet customer expectations and agreed service levels. All processes must be measurable

4. Partners: When designing services, vendors, manufacturers, and suppliers should be considered as they will be utilized to support the service once it is live. (Ashford Global IT, 2016)

- **Six Sigma tools and methodologies** - With Six Sigma, the overall goal is to refine processes so that they contain less than 3.4 defects per million opportunities. In contrast, 3 Sigma equates to 93.32% perfection which equals roughly 65,000 defects per million operation and Four Sigma equates to 99.38% perfection which equals roughly 6,200 defects per million operations. Six Sigma equates to 99.9997% perfection (3.4 defects per million operations). Within this context, defects may include dissatisfaction experienced by the customer, overly long support calls, retouch on a support issue, or any deviation to established SLAs. Note: In 2005 Motorola attributed over $17 billion dollars in savings to Six Sigma projects and initiatives.

Another major goal of Six Sigma is the reduction or waste.

Below I have listed a few of what I consider to be the most important Six Sigma tools and methodologies that can be used by IT managers daily. Note that Six Sigma has many more tools; however, many of them are focused on the area of statistical analysis. I realize that those analysis tools can be of use to a manager, especially when working with data and metrics; but unfortunately, covering them in this text would be too extensive and complex so I have only listed those that I feel are the most easily directed to improving customer service:

1. **QFD** - Quality Function Deployment is a Six Sigma technique for aligning customer wants and requirements with internal processes, projects, and initiatives to assure client needs are met or addressed. It also, by design, calculates the relative importance values across all customer wants to determine where to best focus and prioritize your internal resources to achieve the most value for your customers in an informed fashion. The grid used to perform the analysis (the requirement matrix) can be constructed with a top portion (the correlation matrix) that correlates the internal resources columns with each other - when designed in this fashion it takes on the image of a house, and thus is referred to as the 'House of Quality'. Leveraging this technique is an excellent way to strategically plan service improvements that are based solidly upon customer wants and needs. Note: Templates can be located on the Internet in Excel format to help get you started with your planning

2. **SPC** - Statistical Process Control - is applied to monitor and control process via better understanding of the variances within them. Once variances are noted and tracked, root cause analysis can be used to

determine the cause and a resolution can be then be enacted. The focus with regards to customer service is its ability to spot special causes (resource, equipment, time of day, network segment, etc.) related to variance in processes and address them accordingly

3. **Pareto** - the 80/20 rule (mentioned earlier), states that on average, 80% of the effects (issues) come from 20% of the causes (root problems)

4. **DMAIC** - is a Six Sigma project management methodology that is comprised of 5 separate stages: Define, Measure, Analyze, Improve, and Control

5. **Kano Mode**l - depicts (via its graph) and explains the connection between customer satisfaction and proficiency of requirement fulfillment

6. **VOC** - stands for Voice of the Customer and is a leading concept and consideration with regards to customer satisfaction

7. **CIT** - Critical Incident Technique, is a process for developing surveys that are accurate, timely, and that address the most important customer considerations. It encompasses the VOC

- **What Muda is** - Muda is a Japanese word meaning "futility; pointlessness; uselessness; or wastefulness" - within Lean, it can mean wasted time, space, energy, motion, resources, or processing; it can also mean defects. Generally, Muda means Waste

- **What a SWOT Analysis is** - This is an acronym that stands for Strengths, Weaknesses, Opportunities, and Threats. These terms are usually placed on a 2x2 grid with strengths above opportunities on the left and with weaknesses above threats on the right. With this standard alignment helpful attributes (S, O) would be the vertical left with harmful attributes (W, T) being on the vertical right and internal attributes (S, W) being on the horizontal top and external considerations (O, T) being on the horizontal bottom. With this simple configuration assessments can be performed on all four areas of concern. I will also mention a related but less realized tool - **RIOM** (Risk, Issues, and Opportunity Management). This is a tool that I was introduced to during my time with a relatively large company (who actually sponsored training for it). It is used to assess and mitigate risks, identify, and resolve issues before they become risks, and to spot and weigh opportunities to determine if action should be taken to capitalize on them based on possible benefit versus investment. Although not as popular as some of the other well know tools, it is worth mentioning that it is leveraged by organizations such as NASA and the Department of defense

- **The concept of Cost of Quality** - (see 'Managing Quality Costs' earlier in this chapter).

- **ISO 9001:2015 Seven Quality Management Principles** - The ISO 9001:2015 Quality Management System is based on seven principles from total quality management (TQM). As mentioned earlier, a company keeps clients by providing value; the seven principles are designed and aligned to assure that a company has the ability to both understand what their client's most current perceptions of value are and to make sure that the client consistently receives the value that they expect. These principles, when used together, create a viable quality management system that assures consistency in delivering quality, value, and continuous improvement. These principals are:

  1. **Customer Focus**. Understand the customer's needs, meet the customer's requirements, and strive to exceed the customer's expectations. Note that a customer's expectations are derived from

conversations with your company from the initial sales discussions, through negotiations and contract construction, and the associated SLAs that have been set. The customer will also weight their perception of value on whatever the current industry standards may be.

2.   Leadership. Establishes unity of purpose and organizational direction (Mission, Vision, and Strategic Goals) and provides an environment that promotes employee involvement and achievement of objectives.

3.   Engagement of People. Creating value for your customers will be easier if you have competent, empowered and engaged staff. It is to a company's benefit to take advantage of fully involved employees, using their abilities for the benefit of both the clients and the organization. This is a vital consideration that is often missed by both leadership and management.

4.   Process Approach. It is important to recognize that things accomplished well and consistently are often the results of effective processes and that processes, along with good documentation practices, must be managed. Creating value from well vetted, documented, and repeatable processes is vital to business continuity over time. Processes should also be audited as time passes and operational requirements change.

5.   Continual Improvement. Continual improvement is at the core of just about every quality focused methodology used today and should be a permanent objective applied to the organization and to its people, processes, systems, services, and products (internal facing improvements). Improvement should also be focused on external considerations such as client needs and relationships as well as vendor relationships and performance.

6. **Factual Approach to Decision Making**.
Decisions must be based on the analysis of accurate, relevant, and reliable data and information. Ensuring your decisions are based on these considerations is more likely to produce the most accurate and desired results.

7. **Mutually Beneficial Supplier Relationships**.
Both the organization and the supplier benefiting from one another's role in their relationship. Holding regular conversations with your vendors and suppliers is critical and can lend to better performance, understanding of expectations, and ultimately the end results delivered to your clients. I once read that "you cannot deliver Six Sigma quality to your clients while partnering with Three Sigma vendors" (Goetsch, 01/2012)

- **W. Edwards Deming's 14 Points for Total Quality Management** (critical to exploring and enacting Total Quality Management (TQM):
  1. Create constancy of purpose for improving products and services
  2. Adopt the new philosophy
  3. Cease dependence on inspection to achieve quality
  4. End the practice of awarding business on price alone; instead, minimize total cost by working with a single supplier
  5. Improve constantly and forever every process for planning, production, and service
  6. Institute training on the job

7. Adopt and institute leadership
8. Drive out fear
9. Break down barriers between staff areas
10. Eliminate slogans, exhortations, and targets for the workforce
11. Eliminate numerical quotas for the workforce and numerical goals for management
12. Remove barriers that rob people of pride of workmanship, and eliminate the annual rating or merit system
13. Institute a vigorous program of education and self-improvement for everyone
14. Put everybody in the company to work accomplishing the transformation

Helpful Insight:

Recommendation: Although there are hundreds of books and texts out there, listed below are a few of my favorite books and I recommend that any engaged manager should read when they have time:
1. The Five Dysfunctions of a Team - Patrick Lencioni
2. Common Sense Leadership - Roger Fulton
3. Who Moved My Cheese - Spencer Johnson
4. The Art of War - Sun Tzu
5. The 7 Habits of Highly Effective People - Stephen Covey
6. The Speed of Trust - Stephen Covey
7. Bushido: The Soul of Japan - Inazo Nitobe

As an IT Manager...

My leadership style starts out as situational, as I first come on-board (as I need to evaluate and gain an understanding of the current culture, processes, personalities, and styles, and even my leadership). I then move towards a combination of goal oriented and democratic leadership style as I settle in. However, overall, my leadership style is consistently professional, honest, fair, ethical, supportive, and inspirational.

Democratic Leadership – I chose to adopt this form of leadership style initially as I find it beneficial to collaboration and knowledge transfer with my staff, some of which may have been with the company for years prior to my arriving. It allows for the possibility of making more informed decisions during the initial months. I see this type of leadership as viable as long as in the end the leader makes logical, strategic decisions based on the input and feedback that he or she has received from all his staff, as opposed to selecting the most popular input or suggestion. One positive aspect of democratic leadership is that it involves the employees, their participation, and their input - in contrast to a more autocratic leadership style (which can be perceived as a more oppressive, overbearing, or dictatorial type of leadership). This style leaves room and opportunity for employee empowerment (brainstorming sessions and quality circles) and team building. I would say that of all the leadership styles, this is the style that I tend to adopt the most. I see Bill Gates as being an example of this type of leadership style as he is known for making exceptionally good strategic decisions, having a focus and vision for the future, listens to what customers want, and engaging his employees and strategic alliances.

As mentioned, I tend to balance democratic leadership with goal-oriented leadership. Goal orientated leadership style alone can be a bit short-sighted or constraint. It can possibly cause more harm than good due to its narrow focus on just the goal as opposed to the surrounding impact on people, culture, competing goals and initiatives, and future planning (see balanced score cards). I know of a company that, through changes in management, gradually drifted towards this form of leadership style as a primary style and as a result, what once was a very prosperous and proud company with bright future began to fail. Initiatives were based on saving the here and now with no real planning for mapping out provisioning to support a better future state. In addition, along the transition, core moral considerations were not transmitted or enforced, leading to the ultimate change in direction of the company.

I will also mention the use of Quality Circles - I have used these rather effectively in the past; they are a form of productive teamwork sessions that leverages the joint insight and perspective of individual contributing staff members to develop better solutions. The focus of these meetings has covered everything from customer focus, process enhancements, common issues, to new procedures all together.

Helpful Insight:

My personal core beliefs and cornerstones:
- The core of any company is a combination of the quality of its products or services and its proficiency with the customer service and support related to those products and services
- Always strive to deliver quality service
- Always be honest with customers, clients, staff, and management
- Kaizen: Continually improving all things, at all levels at all times – forever

- A firm belief that employee engagement and empowerment lends to company success
- Always follow the company's strategic goals, guiding principles, direction, and management decisions
- To speak up whenever you feel that an improvement can be made - even if it may not be considered (management should make you feel trusted enough to do so)
- Supporting, motivating, and guiding my team at all times in all things
- A belief in a Total Quality approach to management
- A manager's success is dependent upon his ability to manage a balanced focus on company, client, and staff

Helpful Insight:

My personal philosophies:
- Think ahead, plan ahead, to always be ahead
- Walk the proper paths and you can never go wrong
- To make good decisions you need to make informed decisions
- Logic, Wisdom, Maturity, Focus, and Professionalism – Always

Final note:
I see a company's value to its clients as being driven by Quality, Performance, Professionalism, Timeliness, Honesty, Integrity, and innovativeness – great service with great customer service and support, led by great leadership will always captivate your clients.

Levin J. Allen

CHAPTER 2

Focus on the Staff

As an IT manager with the responsibility of managing staff associated with service and support, it is essential to be able to effectively build and manage groups of people that will not only need to work well together as a team but are able to interact well with clients. This ability is critical to client satisfaction and day to day business continuity. Staff management is one of the many interconnected components of business operations that has the capability to affect any other area that it directly or indirectly touches.

As a manager of people for many years, I have developed a methodology and philosophy for managing my staff in two distinct directions, in that I address and manage them separately (by treating each as an individual) and I address and manage them together as a group (by providing for them holistically and encouraging them to work together as a team). The team mentality is especially important when it comes to finding solutions to support and service issues and problems. In these cases, I do my best to embed in them the value of being able to form a 'hive' mentality.

In treating each of my staff as an individual, I get to know more about their unique qualities, what drives and motivates them, what their individual issue or concerns may be, even what frustrates them. I focus on establishing a one-on-one rapport with each. I find this to be critical regarding staff engagement, overall communication and awareness, and culture building.

In encouraging teamwork, I try to promote a think-tank mentality whereas each individual is comfortable with reaching out to another if they need an answer, assist, or guidance. This is up and above the use of knowledge bases that are maintained and accessible via the support system. This behavior is essential to building the hive mentality I mentioned earlier, where capability sits across the entire team. This benefits the client as well as continuously educates the weaker members of the team via the continuous knowledge transfer. Over time more and more of a team mentality exists and the stronger the team is as a whole and as individuals. My only caution with this approach is if all or most of the team tend to lean too heavily on one or two top resources to the degree that it can hinder their productivity. In those cases, making sure that the top resources are updating the knowledge bases may help with knowledge transfer or it may bear out the necessity for additional training across the most deficient lines of knowledge within the team. Deficiencies can also be analyzed by logging what areas tend to be the most problematic to your team over time - this involves good communications with your team and the appropriate metrics to monitor. This "team think-tank" approach also lends to both capability management and capacity management over time.

On recruiting resources:

One of the core responsibilities of a good manager is to be able to both recruit and retain a highly effective and efficient team of resources (engineers, admins, technicians, etc.). This process starts at the beginning.

When hiring a new resource, it is important to not just assess the candidate's experience and training; his or her character, passions, maturity, professionalism, style, and even experiences play an important role in how effectively he or she will perform overall. This is especially important if you, as the hiring manager, are paying attention to your department's culture, team dynamics, and impact with regards to client contact. He or she must not only be aware of what is technically going on around them but culturally and professionally as well. They should also be mindful of the client's perceptions and the impact of any negative impressions they may make as well.

Your expectations regarding professionalism, maturity, lateness, routinely calling off unexpectedly, growth over time, and other high-level concerns need to be mentioned and discussed during the interview stage.

An effective manager needs to plant the seeds of culture and expectations early. For them to bloom they must be consistently nurtured. Nurturing can be established by consistency of message, leading by example, keeping the message prevalent within communications and meetings, praising its support, and correcting non-conformance.

This is important when adding a new resource to the team. I recall an incident when one of my earlier teams was very well tuned and all sat comfortably within the quality culture that was being built. However, during the on boarding of a new engineer (that I was not involved with hiring), who was senior and was looked up to by the younger tech staff. I noticed that he tended to be somewhat crass and swore a lot (possibly in an attempt to seem cool, cavalier, or inveterate). I noticed over the course of the next few weeks that several other engineers started cursing when speaking with him as well - this got to the point where it became fairly commonplace, did not seem to be waning, and to the degree where I began to have concerns that these conversations may be overheard by clients on the phone during a support call.

To curtail this issue without calling out anyone in particular, I sent out a general email to the staff one morning reminding them how our culture was important, that I have been hearing a lot of swearing, mentioned how our offices should remain professional for the sake of all staff as well as visitors that my stop in. I also mentioned my concern of the conversations being inadvertently overheard by a client on the phone and the impression that it would send. In the email I also thank them for their professional attitudes and approach and that it has always been greatly appreciated. The issue vanished that day and never resurfaced. This reinforced the adage that I have always shared with my teams that "who we are is us..." (See chapter 5 on Culture)

As mentioned, it is important to assess a potential team member on their professionalism, maturity, and soft skills as well as on their technical experience, skill sets, and training. Vetting these qualities early will help avoid conduct issues, client communications issues, and negative team impact after bringing a resource on-board. It is much preferable to assess and possibly avoid a problem piece before hiring than to need to spend countless hours addressing, correcting, or possibly removing it afterward.

Historically, I have opted to bring in a resource with good soft skills and good technical skills over a candidate with slightly better technical skills but very bad soft skills. Note this is only when the candidate's technical skills meets or exceeds the demands of the position as matching technical ability to position and service delivery requirements is imperative. If necessary, and if you are able to, interview until you have a candidate that fills both requirements reasonably well. Note: This may, and most likely will, prolong the hiring process; however, the position gets filled with the best candidate as opposed to a candidate selected due to time constraints that may not fit or last. Also note that the time required to locate a suitable candidate can be minimized by having a very close relationship with your recruiter. This is to make sure that they are aware of the detailed specifics of skill sets, education, and experience that you are looking for and are only sending candidates to your door that fill those requirements. This will reduce the number of bad candidates that show up and help with acquiring an appropriate resource quicker. Performing this degree of vetting by the recruiter and by yourself reflects the age-old adage "measure twice to only need to cut once".

Helpful Insight:

A few standard non-technical interview questions:
Below are a few of the non-technical questions that I would add to the technical questions that are being asked during an interview. Not all may be used, however a few may be added just to help gain some insight of the individual's soft skills.

- How would you define customer service? This gives me some idea if the candidate has any idea of what customer service is all about - it may reflect their experiences, training, or just their lack of exposure to the concept. I would expect lack of exposure more from a candidate for a junior position than I would when filling a senior technician position

- What would you say are the top 3 things that lend to client satisfaction? This is similar to the first question but gives me a more specific understanding of the candidates basic understanding of what lends to keeping our, or any, clients happy in this arena of business. Good answers would be along the lines of fast response, first pass resolution, professionalism, or timely and clear communications. Answers that would cause some concern would be "I don't know" or "I'm not sure"

- Can you tell me a few of your problem-solving methodologies? This helps me to understand how they have historically addressed problems, if they have good methodologies or a good sense of how to drill down on an issue - such as isolating variables, determining the scope of the problem by determining who is impacted and who is not, checking for a possible trigger event, or attempting to locate a root cause. This gives some idea of how they may perform on a support call, what training or supervision they may need, and as before, expectations regarding their answer are greater with more advanced positions

- What do you know about this company? My hopes are that anyone vying for a position would have taken the time to look up and learn a little about the company they are attempting to become a part of. If anything, it demonstrates the company itself bears some importance to them and that they are not just looking to secure a position just anywhere without concern or insight regarding the company itself. It also bears out that they are forward thinking and inclined to think ahead and prepare in advance

- What drew you to this position / what interests you about this position? This is to gain some insight on how they matched themselves to the position and what prompted them to submit their resume. There have been times where the answers to this question were very enlightening

- How do you handle multiple deadlines? The answer to this question can lend insight to their sense of priority, triage, logical thinking, escalation, communication, and consideration

- What do you feel are the top 3 qualities that you possess that qualify you for this position? This will help to reinforce what I may have seen as their top contributing factors from reading their resume or even bring to light qualities that had not theretofore been mentioned. Either way, it lets me know how they feel about their qualities and abilities and what they feel they're most efficient at

- Knowing the position, do you foresee any challenges if hired? This is the opposite of the previous question and provides a point of disclosure for anything not mentioned during the discussion or on their resume that may possible be problematic later, if they are hired
- What would you say is the biggest IT challenge you have faced and how did you handle it? This is usually only asked of senior technicians and provides a point for them to showcase what they may feel to be shining moments in their careers - it can often lend insights to their resourcefulness and agility
- What are a few of the traits that you liked about your favorite manager and what are some of the traits that you did not like about your worst manager? This provides a bit of early, general insight on what works for them and what does not regarding management or their experiences, both good and bad. The answers to this question are usually reasonable; however, it is good to see the degree of candor that some candidates display

Moving on

Now that you have taken the time and effort to bring in the best talent, on-board them, and train them and you have integrated them into the culture and have introduced them to the clients - it is time to focus on 'Performance' and 'Retention'.

On Performance:

A staff member's performance is based on several factors, some of which they personally have direct control over and some which they do not. A few of the things that a person does have control over is their focus, effort and determination, dedication to learn and grow, capacity to do the right things at the right times for the right reasons, attendance, desire to do their best, and ability to be honest with both themselves and their managers. This may also subliminally extend to their tenacity, courage, moral compass, and decision-making skills.

A few of the factors that you, as a manager, control that greatly lend to a staff member's performance are providing clear instructions, providing the appropriate training, providing an environment that is at the very least comfortable and easy to work in, providing the necessary tools with which to perform the required tasks effectively, providing guidance and support, and providing good leadership.

Basically, an individual's overall performance is a mix of what they are able to control and what you, as their manager are able to control. I mention this because it is important to bear this in mind during performance reviews - that you take the time before meeting with them to determine what impact you may have had on their performance and that the factors that they are being assessed on are all under their ability to control. It also allows you to discuss items that you control and will work with them on, to help improve their performance between reviews. I see this as both fair and reasonable.

Training is also a vary essential aspect of performance that needs to take place from day one on the job – starting with the introduction to the relevant systems, processes, policies, procedures, protocols, and people that will need to be understood to become productive and fully functional as an integrated gear in the machinery of day-to-day operations.

It is also important to make sure that they do not fall into the usual traps of day-to-day operations due to rushing, taking short-cuts, ignoring danger signs, proceeding without certainty, or even just stopping at question marks and not proceeding because they just do not know (see below).

Teach them to:

- Not to just stop at a question mark - there have been many of occasions where I would discover that a task was not performed, or issue examined based on an answer that started with "I didn't know..." This is the thinking behind the Japanese business philosophy of 'Genchi Genbutsu' - which roughly translated to "go and see" or "to go to the actual place". There is also an English adage which similarly states that "When in doubt, check it out"

- Focus on and work more towards discovering and resolving root causes as opposed to focusing on eliminating reported symptoms – especially with multiple reports of an issue reported day after day or an issue affecting a specific group. The thought that needs to be triggered is "Why does this keep happening". This philosophy falls under both the Pareto Principle and ITIL incident and problem management best practices

- Not to proceed from a supposition or uncertainty - This is another issue that I have found can be very prevalent and comfortably absorbed within a department or company. You can tell that this issue is present when you continually hear the terms "Well, it used to be that...", "I believe that...", "yes that should be...", "I think that...", or any number of similar non-definitive statements given when someone is giving an answer to an inquiry or direct question. This comfortable adoption of the passage of 'Possibly Inaccurate' information can lead to so many additional problems downstream that it can be considered a direct contributor to poor quality costs.

- Slow down - I am known for telling my teams to "Measure twice to only need to cut once" - it may be an old adage, but it makes logical sense as does the saying "Haste makes waste". Being in a hurry is what locks your keys in the house or gets you a speeding ticket and only serves to delay your intended goal (whatever it was that you were attempting to expedite by rushing). Unfortunately, within the IT service and support arena, it also leads to the need to revisit a solution that did not work the first time around because time was not taken to check it (retouch), lends to client frustration, and lends to poor quality costs.

- Be empathetic - to see things from the client's point of view. Bring the service staff closer to the client perspective via training and awareness. Ask them about their personal experiences, times when they expected quality for something that they paid for and did not receive it - how did they feel at that moment, and did they ever use that product or service again?

- Learn as they go: One of the things that I admire about level 3 service and support engineers is their ability to face the unknown every day. I realize that they are well trained and have a good degree of experience; however, even the most experienced technicians will run into a situation that they have never encountered before. Their ability to assess, analyze, and resolve those theretofore unexperienced issues is what truly exhibits their skill. Not only does this ability lend to client satisfaction due to reduced resolution time, but it also lends to the technician by adding to his acumen and experience. This being said, they should never hit the same tripwire twice because once they have hit it, they know where it is and hopefully have removed or disarmed it and documented it for future reference

- To understand the dynamics of the business - this helps them to manage self-induced stress, which can sit on top of the regular everyday stresses that come with being within a service and support arena. I once had an admin mention to me that he was frustrated because there were often when speaking with a client that no matter how helpful he attempted to be the client still remained angry and upset. He mentioned that it, in turn, ruins his good mood and his day. I mentioned to him 2 things that help him to address that issue moving forward without frustration or consternation - these 2 things were: (a) Encountering upset clients is inherent to service and support, our jobs are to minimize the occurrences by listening, learning, and fixing whatever the issue is that is upsetting the client and, if applicable, making sure that no one else encounters it afterward. In that way, every reported issue is an opportunity for us to satisfy a client and to possibly get stronger. As long as we receive complaints well, complaints are the exception and not the rule, and we grow from them - we are on the proper path. (b) Sometimes your efforts will not be received well - and that is fine because the honor is in your honest effort to console and help; that honesty, due diligence, and effort can only leave a positive impression - even on a negative mind. Even if not during the call, the impression that you make will linger in that person's mind when they calm down. This is especially true if the issue is resolved in a timely manner and you follow up with them to make sure that they are OK.

On Retention:

After a resource has been on your team for a while and has been learning and performing well, clients begin to become comfortable seeing them, relying on them, and working with the same resource over time. This gives the client the comfort and value-add associated with familiarity and with past performance. If the client loses a resource that has demonstrated itself to be both effective and efficient with regards to service delivery, as well professional, likable, and personable, then the value that the client received regarding stability, reliability, and security of knowing that they are in good hands is removed. This tends to greatly upset clients. Even worse, recurrence of this issue greatly erodes the client's confidence in your company's ability to govern and control itself, let alone their concerns.

Another aspect of maintaining, and retaining, an astute technical staff is the value of "ground level" perspective of the client's infrastructure as well as insights on their expressed thoughts and concerns with regards to day-to-day operations, possible infrastructure changes, or future planning. Within IT management, your admins, engineers, and technicians are usually at ground-level with your client's infrastructure and are the best resources for watching, listening, and reporting for current or potential future issues. This level of situational awareness provides you the opportunity to be proactive with support initiatives or even pro-actively offer additional services that would legitimately curtail pending issues and to mitigate potential risks for the client.

A third consideration regarding retention is the retention of knowledge, experience, and familiarity with a client's infrastructure - past state, current state, and even the transitional states over time. Consider what occurs when a tenured engineer who has worked with a specific client for several years decides to leave the company because he or she is not happy with their manager or the company in general. According to an article recently written on Forbes.com, "What's especially poignant is that it's easier to keep your employees happy than to make them mad. To keep your employees happy to work on your team, all you have to do is treat them the way you'd like to be treated yourself." (Ryan, 2017)

Also, loss of revenue can stem from (a) sudden capacity loss that causes service levels to fall below contractual SLAs, (b) cascade failure with other staff due to their attempts to fill the capacity void created by the resource that suddenly left, (c) the cost for recruitment, replacement, on-boarding, and training of a replacement resource (which can often take 2-6 months), (d) what I consider as '**regroup/rediscovery time**' associated with attempting to regain knowledge, information, or insight that left the company in the head of the engineer who suddenly departed - without off-boarding, knowledge transfer, or opportunity to document that which has not been. This is one good reason to have processes in place for documenting every aspect of a client's infrastructure and its changes over time and maintaining strict policies and procedures relating to knowledge and document management).

This reminds me of a time when I worked for a company that had 6 engineers; however, there was 1 engineer who was with the company for over 10 years, knew just about everything about every client's infrastructure (as he was involved with just about every aspect of their technical buildouts) and thus held an excellent rapport with just about every client. He also possessed an exceptional memory and was able to hold information in his head regarding just about every client, down to the finest of detail. After being with the company for a short while I realized that there were times when other engineers could not perform the tasks required for support of some of the key clients unless they asked the lead engineer what the process, procedure, current state, or other key information was. This was because he often kept some of this information in his head and a lot of it was not documented anywhere. Apparently, there was never enough time and he would get to it, eventually. I recall thinking at the time, what would happen if this particular engineer hit the lottery and literally left the company over night. I subsequently requested that he takes to the time to shore up all current information that was undocumented regarding client sites. Note, this lends to considerations related to IT operations knowledge bases, document management systems, and well vetted and enforced policies.

Helpful Insight:

My 5 steps for effective, and efficient staff management:
1.   Hire for professionalism, maturity, and character as well as for technical expertise and set expectations early in the interviewing process

2.   Consistently deliver clear and unambiguous instructions (guide rails to keep all on the same, correct tracks)

3.   Hold each individual accountable - not conceding to any other considerations - this is done in a

respectful, business-centric fashion as opposed to belligerently or harshly. It is simply assuring that they are performing the tasks that they have been hired to perform

4.   Actively try to help to improve problematic personnel to become stronger and more engaged. This is a manager's due diligence regarding staff efficiency and retention. Up and above that it is up to the staff member to strive to operate efficiently and effectively

5.   If attempts to help fail - follow standard HR steps for astutely documenting and logging all warnings, meetings, communications, and attempts to illicit change and move towards termination and replacement with a more viable resource if improvement does not occur.

Along with this I attempt to maintain an open-door policy, meet with my team as individuals during one-on-one meetings as well as regular team meetings and continuously let them know that I am there for them as much as I am for the company and the client. I also regularly convey a simple sentiment to my teams that goes as follows - 'What we are is comprised of us - how we treat each other and how we work together as a team. That defines our culture and that greatly contributes to our successes'.

"Gallup also found that engagement is highest among employees who have some form (face to face, phone or digital) of daily communication with their managers. Managers who use a combination of face-to-face, phone and electronic communication are the most successful in engaging employees." (Gallup Inc., 2015)

As mentioned, vetting a candidate's character helps to mitigate the risk of rapid turn-over due to un-vetted issues early on. The recommendation is to apply a degree of scrutiny and consideration during hiring – the goal is not to find the perfect candidate, as this may be impossible due to the combination of viable attributes can be endless. The benefit is in becoming somewhat aware of the person that you intend to bring into your team, let into your systems, and allowing to face your clients. It is beneficial to be able to spot and curtail any potentials problem areas as early as possible and making a more informed, and possibly viable, decision from there.

Understand them:

If your role as an IT manager includes the responsibility of managing IT staff (engineers, admins, or technicians), I guarantee that over time you will be exposed to a very wide range of personalities, characters, styles, and attitudes - some of which will be incredibly unique and intriguing to say the least. Regarding this aspect of people management, I will say that having a basic understanding of human nature and psychology would be beneficial to your ability to manage a diverse set of individuals. A measure of insight or training in this regard can only lend to your ability to transform the "Group" that you may ultimately be responsible for into a comprehensive, unified "Team". You should be able to gain a practical degree of understanding by researching and through studying basics human psychology, sociology, business psychology, management science, or other areas within the behavioral sciences. Acumen can and will also be achieved over time and exposure to situations involving directly working with and paying attention to people. If you are relatively new to management, I would suggest taking a basic course in human psychology or class /seminar on people management.

"Business Psychology which is also known as Organizational or Industrial Psychology concerns the application of psychological theories, research methods, and intervention strategies to workplace issues. Business psychologists are interested in making organizations more productive while ensuring workers are able to lead physically and psychologically healthy lives. Other relevant concerns include personnel psychology, motivation and leadership, employee selection, training and development, organization development, organizational behavior, workplace and family issues." - (Masood)

It would also be helpful to gain some understanding of the basic functions and considerations of the Human Resources department – this will be especially useful when dealing with problematic staff situations that may need to be escalated.

There are also several mainstream tools, tests, surveys, and insights related to understanding the people that you manage - a few were mentioned in the previous chapter for management (see Parkinson's Law and the Yerkes–Dodson law in chapter 1). Beyond those, there are a few additional tests that are traditionally use by employers, HR departments, and consultants. The tools that I have been exposed to over time and am the most familiar with are:

The Thomas-Kilmann Conflict Mode Instrument (TKI) - This tool addresses how individuals tend to handle conflict, that is, it is designed to assess a person's behavior in conflict situations. It is a tool that can be used to better understand how an individual's predisposition for managing conflicts can impact business continuity and team dynamics.

The Thomas Kilmann Conflict Mode Instrument begins by identifying the two basic dimensions of Conflict Behavior:

Assertiveness: The degree to which you try to satisfy your own concerns during a conflict. This is related to how you might try to meet your needs or receive support for your ideas.

Cooperativeness: The degree to which you try to satisfy the other individuals' concerns. It is related to how you might try to help the other individual meet his or her needs or how you can be receptive to the other individuals' ideas (Thomas 3-4).

The TKI assessment applies the basic two dimensions of Assertiveness and Cooperativeness to the five conflict-handling modes to create the five major combinations possible in a conflict situation, which are described as:

Competing: Is assertive and uncooperative. In this mode, you try to satisfy your own concerns at the other person's expense.

Collaborating: Is both assertive and cooperative. In this mode, you try to find a win-win solution that completely satisfies the concerns of both individuals involved.

Compromising: Is intermediate in both assertiveness and cooperativeness. In this mode, you try to find an acceptable solution that only partially satisfies both individual's concerns.

Avoiding: Is both unassertive and uncooperative. In this mode, you work to sidestep the conflict without attempting to satisfy either individual's concerns.

Accommodating: Is unassertive and cooperative. In this mode, you try to satisfy the other person's concerns at the expense of your own concerns. (Thomas, 2002)

Chally Test - This test is often used by employers when they are seeking to obtain a fairly valid assessment of an individual's ability to perform the job that they are vying for. The Chally test is designed to measure the competencies, acumen, adaptability, and other job performance behaviors based on the statistical analysis of their assessment test scores. I have taken this test in the past and found it to be extremely precise in its ability to accurately assess a person's fundamental character and performance attributes. Many of you may have taken this test yourselves in the past - given by HR of your present company of the hiring manager of a company you were looking to join.

Myers Briggs - is a personality test that is often used by HR or the hiring manager to assess a potential new hire.

All of the above-mentioned tests and instruments are designed to help you better understand the psychology, personality, or character of your current or potential staff. They serve to give you a better idea of what is happening "underneath the hood" if you will.

Lastly, with regards to this topic, I will mention that as a people manager, gaining insight into human behavior regarding how to "read" people via proven and universally accepted methods, and understanding the related social psychology concepts can provide you with an edge when it comes to managing your relationships with your staff as well as with your clients. There are literally hundreds of sites on the Internet that you can access for free in your spare time to gain especially useful insight on this topic. Insights that, if you were not aware of before researching, can lend great value-add with your ability to better manage effective communications and relationship building. Below is a brief synopsis regarding this topic from just one such site:

Common errors people make in reading people:

Ignoring context: Crossed arms do not mean much if the room is cold or the chair, they are sitting in does not have armrests. Everything must pass the commonsense test given the environment. So, ask yourself: "Should someone in this situation be acting like this?"

Not looking for clusters: One of the biggest errors you make is looking for one single tell. That is great in movies about poker players but in real life it is a consistent grouping of actions (sweating, touching the face, and stuttering together) that is really going to tell you something. So, ask yourself: "Are most of this person's behaviors associated with X?"

Not getting a baseline: If someone is always jumpy, jumpiness doesn't tell you anything. If someone is always jumpy and they suddenly stop moving -- HELLO. So, ask yourself: "Is this how they normally act?"

Not being conscious of biases: If you already like or dislike the person, it is going to affect your judgment. And if people compliment you, are similar to you, are attractive... these can all sway you, unconsciously. (I know, I know, you do not fall for those tricks. Well, the biggest bias of all is thinking you are unbiased.) - (Dreeke, 2016)

Guide them:

It seems to me that this is one of the most important aspects of team building and staff management that is most often forgotten or not implemented. This may possibly be due to the lack of understanding of the importance associated with this strategic requirement for building and retaining an effective team. My belief tends to be supported by the tone of feedback supplied by employees on popular review sites such as glassdoor.com and indeed.com. In reading through the reviews of the companies that received the lowest ratings by current and past staff, the most prominent reason given for someone leaving the company involves their direct manager or management in general.

Guiding your team well allows for not only better staff retention, but a better ability to leverage your team effectively and achieve your company's business and financial goals. Look at it this way - in a sense, your team is your army, your "ground level troops", you are their commander, and the company owns the army - if you do not provide adequate guidance to your troops they will fail to deliver when they are needed to complete critical, tactical tasks. Applicable to both sides of this analogy are tasks such as situational assessment, recon, beating their competition, or general day to day front-line operations. Without proper guidance they will not know how to adequately perform the required tasks in relations to the company's strategic planning. During a battle, there would be no coordinated effort or adherence to strategic planning or execution of clear and cohesive instructions - they could end up all over the battlefield running about Willy-Nilly. The odds of you winning any battle (achieving your company's goals and objectives) in this case are extremely against you.

If you look up the definition of 'Guide', you will find definitions along the lines of: 'one that leads or directs another's way'. This definition represents your responsibility, your duty, to your staff. If they are to be expected to do well, to perform well, they will need the guidance and attention of their direct manager. Once again, this is an area that is often missed and the results are staff that feel ignored, uncertain, abandoned, set up for failure, frustrated, and in a lot of cases fed up and looking for better opportunities.

This is not a difficult task for any manager to perform, it just takes awareness of the responsibility, a good degree of leadership ability, genuine care, and knowledge (best practices, understanding people, etc.). If you have read this far in this book, and if you did not know before, you are now aware of the responsibility and value-add. You should have some sense of your specific level of leadership ability (via past experience, training, natural inclination, or a combination of all three). Regarding genuine care – If you do not genuinely care about your team or the position you hold, then honestly, you should not be in the position. As for knowledge - this is a combination of what you bring to the table (the personal experiences and acumen that you have collected over the years), what you are able to become situational aware of while on-boarding, and what you come to understand as you grow into and with the position.

Teams, people, tend to comfortably follow those who they feel are capable, knowledgeable, and will lead them in good directions. Good guidance is comprised of supplying good answers and being able to point them towards the best and most honorable, informative, secure, and empowering paths. As a manager, you were once where your team members are today; however, over time you have gained the experience, insight, and acumen that has risen you to the level of manager. Now is the time to leverage that knowledge and information to provide good guidance to those who can benefit from it as they strive to grow and develop professionally as you have, and in some cases help them gain personal growth as well.

Guidance is one of the most important core considerations of some of the most prestigious institutions on the planet. One such institution is the U.S. Marines. Within this institution's leadership principles, it is said that a leader should "...know your Marines and how they react to different situations. This knowledge can save lives. A Marine who is nervous and lacks self-confidence should never be put in a situation where an important, instant decision must be made. Knowledge of your Marines' personalities will enable you, as the leader, to decide how to best handle each Marine and determine when close supervision is needed." - (Air University, 2014)

It is amazing how closely this sentiment echoes the requirements of a team leader in the IT service venue. Fact: Service and support resources (engineers, administrators, technicians, etc.) come in an endless variety of attributes - male, female, young, old, experienced, not so experienced, introverted, extroverted, subtle, belligerent, recalcitrant, honest, deceitful, honed, raw, and a dozen other primary variants on personality traits and styles. These traits are coupled with various moods, habits, predilections, idiosyncrasies, and possible individual psychological and social tendencies. The range extends from those who are new to the venue and unsure of themselves to those who are tenured, well informed and see themselves as invaluable. From those who shy away from responsibility and perform the bare minimal effort to those who you will need to rein in because they are overly enthusiastic to the degree that they are counterproductive. This is one of the reasons that I mentioned earlier in this chapter that it is important to vet your candidates well and early - as that junction can be your best opportunity regarding ease of management of that individual downstream. It is also why I have mentioned that it is important to know your staff as individuals.

It is also why it is important to have some degree of understanding of human nature, human psychology, and to go through some level of management training - the rest of your acumen builds with experience over time.

Another aspect of guidance that IT Management shares with the Marines is the development of a sense of teamwork within its constituents. This is also another area where the understanding of personality traits comes in handy. Some engineers are naturally inclined to work alone as opposed as in groups - others are worried that sharing what they know can be a detriment to their personal viability. Understanding these personality traits is vital to being able to help these individuals overcome these constraints and to form viable, cohesive teams. One tactic that The Marines uses is creating situations during training where individuals learn the value of working together via actual experience. They have training that allow the recruits to tackle several segments of a course independently; however, there are elements of the course that requires teamwork for the group to pass - effectively transforming a group of unrelated recruits (similar to what you may start off with or inherit as an IT manager) into an effective team. The training teaches the recruits how to survive as a team as well as teaches the value and necessity of teamwork in the field.

I do not suggest or advocate you running your team through military survival drills; however, I do feel that it is important to stress the point that (a) you, as a manager of people, will come across and need to manage and lead a diverse group of individuals, (b) it is important to understand that each individual has his or her unique proclivities, (c) it is important to be able to spot, overcome, and bring all of the diverse constituents together to form an effective team, and (d) in doing so, you will positively impact the performance, proficiency, and moral of your team as well as increase overall operational efficiency and client satisfaction.

Lead them:

To be succinct, either you have what it takes or have the desire to learn what it takes to be an effective leader built into you as a person, or you do not. Only you can honestly assess this truth.

What I can tell you is that over the annals of time, many have cited what it takes to be a good leader. These citations have included leaders of nations, leaders of rebellions, leaders of corporations, leaders of movements, leaders of armies, and more. If you take the time to examine which traits over time tend to be consistent among all the great, renowned, and celebrated leaders, you may come up with a list similar to this - They tend to be:

- Honorable
- Benevolent
- Honest
- Brave
- Visionaries
- Driven by rectitude
- Morally regulated
- Focused on the needs of their followers
- Insightful
- Self-reflective
- Caring
- Passionate
- Determined
- In most cases, charismatic

You can take a moment to weigh yourself against this list - based on your past actions, your current thinking, what others have said of you, and what you feel in your heart. If you do not match everything in the list, that is fine - if you have the desire to grow and improve yourself, this provides you with an opportunity for reflection and provides solid focal points for improvement – this, in itself, could be deemed honorable, so you can check it off the list.

Levin J. Allen

CHAPTER 3

Focus on the Client

Value

First and foremost, it is important to mention that a client's perception of "value", as both a noun and a verb, needs to be understood, met, and if possible - exceeded.

Basically, to a client or customer, value means: "I have paid my hard-earned money for this particular good or service and expect to receive something of equal or greater importance to me in return". If, in their perception, the return is of equal importance then the value is fair. However, if in their perception the return is of greater importance then the value is considered good or even great. I realize that this is a very rudimentary denotation or explanation of 'Value'; however, I feel that starting at a basic level leaves little room for misinterpretation in this regard.

If you look up the definition of the word Value in the dictionary, you will come across definitions that are similar to:

As a noun:
- The monetary worth of something
- A fair return or equivalent in goods, services, or money for something exchanged
- Relative worth, utility, or importance

As a verb:
- To consider or rate highly (such as in "he values your opinion")

- To estimate or assign the monetary worth of / to appraise (such as in "I value this vase at 1 million dollars")
- To rate or scale in usefulness, importance, or general worth

Given the importance of money within our culture and often, for most of us, difficulties with receiving and accumulating it, whenever it needs to be relinquished for something in return the concept of value is first and foremost in all of our minds. As a noun initially and then more as a verb later, during assessment of the trade. This is usually based on elements such as stability, reliability, or how well it matches up to the expectation of usefulness or functionality; or can be based on any other number of personally imposed parameters.

To bear this out right here right now, take a moment to think about the last 2 or three purchases that you have made and what you think of the value that you received. This can be a meal, a coat, a pair of shoes, or that new gadget that you saw on TV and just had to have; or a service such as plumbing, painting, or tax return preparation. In some cases, such as with a meal at a new restaurant, we may determine that the value far exceeded our expectations (such as with the statement - "wow, I was not expecting so much spaghetti and the meatballs were delicious - I will definitely be coming back and will bring a friend"). And in some cases we may not find that the value met our expectations (such as in the statement "I thought that having my living room and dining room painted for 500 dollars would be a bargain; however, the painter painted over the light fixtures, got paint from the walls on the ceiling, and left the masking tape around the windows when he left - I will not be using him again and would not recommend him to a friend").

The point that I am leading to is that each and every one of us will (1) assess the value of whatever it is that we have paid our hard-earned money for (2) each one of us will determine whether or not we received the expected value, and (3) (most importantly to your business) each of us will decide, based on our assessment, whether or not we will ever make that investment again - let alone recommend.

As an IT service manager, the establishment and understanding of how value is being perceived by your clients is critical to the success of your company. How likely it will be that your client's perceptions will be positive promulgates from elements directly tied to client focused planning, attention to quality, staff ability and engagement, and the effectiveness and efficiency of your processes and procedures.

Quality:
A leading component of perceived value is quality.

Definitions of quality - as a noun:
- An inherent feature (the quality of the diamond was extraordinary)
- Degree of excellence: grade (The beef that we serve is of Grade A quality)
- A distinguishing attribute: (Our past president possesses many fine qualities)

The assessment of quality by customers is a constant in business and holds true regardless of whether a company is big or small and are as equally relevant and applicable to any enterprise ranging from an eight-year-old entrepreneur's lemon aid stand to Microsoft.

Although there is no universally accepted definition of quality across products and services, enough similarity does exist among the definitions that common elements can be extracted:

■Quality involves meeting or exceeding customer expectations

■Quality applies to products, services, people, processes, support, and environments

■Quality is an ever-changing state (i.e., what is considered quality today may not be good enough to be considered quality tomorrow). (Goetsch, 2012)

Innovation

If you are familiar with the Kano Model – and by now you should be (mentioned in chapter 1) - you should notice that one of the most relevant aspects of the model is that it is continually being driven forward by both competition and innovation. Innovation is an important factor with regards to continually delivering what the client considers as quality – and thus their perception of value – over time.

One good example of how vitally important is to constantly keep innovation in mind with regards to your company's growth and stability is how Apple was able to make a comeback in the 80s with the development and introduction of its innovative design for the original Apple iMac. The introduction of the sleek new shape, translucent case, integrated display, and available colors captured the markets attention and helped to bring the company back from the brink. Customers saw the move from the standard rectangular box with a clunky square monitor attached by a cable as innovative, attractive, and of great value to own. This innovative initiative literally saved the company. However, other companies of the time, such as Osborne Computers as well as companies such as Tandy Computers and Commodore (who held 16% and 10 % of the market share respectively in the mid-80s) were not as innovative and forward thinking and were forced into bankruptcy or to move out of the computer manufacturing arena all together. This illustrates how innovation and astute planning, research, analysis, and projections (all based on current and future customer wants and needs) can make the difference between success and going out of business.

One positive aspect of technology and innovation is that unlike a majority of most goods and services over time, innovation with technology can actually reduce the costs to consumers - because it traditionally costs less to produce and deliver. Ultimately, the consumer either gets more technology power or capability for their investment, prices for new versions of technology drops, or a combination of both. For example, 10 years ago a 1 terabyte hard drive cost around $400.00; today you can purchase a 1 terabyte hard drive for less than $50.00. Conversely, today the same $400.00 would cover the cost of a 600-terabyte hard drive.

Another industry that is continually focused on innovation in an attempt to capture the customer's attention is the Auto industry. Innovation driven by competition started around the time that Cadillac founder Henry Leland incorporates electronic starters into their production models in 1912. This innovation represented great value to auto owners at the time, especially those who traditionally needed to use a hand crank to get their vehicles started. Cadillac was also the first auto manufacturer to provide the feature that enables the vehicles lights to stay on after turning off the vehicle engine. Even today, there is a Cadillac commercial showcasing what it calls 'Perfect Position Seating' – an innovative articulating seat architecture with dozens of points for individual adjustments from head to knee to allow the driver to customize his driving experience precisely to his or her proportions and comfort levels. Because of the company's consistent attention to being innovative over time, when you think Cadillac, you think quality.

Today, within the auto industry you can find hundreds of examples of design enhancements driven by innovation, such as rear hatches on minivans that can be opened by passing your foot under the back end of the vehicle, windshield wipers that automatically start at the onset of rain, sensors that warn you if you are drifting out of your lane, rear view cameras are pretty much a standard anymore, the integration of Wi-Fi, Blue Tooth, and ports to allow you to power your ubiquitous mobile devices, and even technology that allows the car to park itself or stop itself if it senses an imminent collision. In addition, corporations such as Uber, Google, Tesla, and BMW are currently working on the development of self-driving cars.

This degree of attention to developing and offering something new to consumers to increase value and/or quality and to beat out the competition is the life blood for most major companies today.

"Automakers invested nearly $105 billion globally on research and development in 2015, ranking the auto industry ahead of other technology-driven industries, including the software/Internet industry and the entire global aerospace and defense industry." (Alliance of Automobile Manufacturers, 2018)

These examples alone should bear out the importance of innovation with regards to growing a business and with a business keeping its clients satisfied, loyal, and away from the competition.

The bottom line - as a business leader with some degree of influence with regards to company projects, initiatives, and development, it is vital to ask yourself a couple of questions:

(a) How can our products or services make our customer's lives better, easier, more productive, or more exciting, and (b) what can we offer that our competitors do not?

Innovation is dependent on and supported by technology and is driven by competition.

The Voice of the Customer (VOC)

As mentioned in chapter 1, the voice of the customer identifies the customer's needs and expectations of your company's products or services. This being said, it is important to have some idea of how to listen for and elicit the thoughts and perceptions of your clients. A few ways for capturing the VOC are:

Via the phone - A random call can provide valuable insight, provide the client the opportunity to mention something that has been on their mind but has not mentioned, and demonstrates a genuine interest and concern regarding the client's well-being.

Via an email – An email requesting feedback on performance and experience can be sent out individually or en masse (with blind cc). The email can contain just a general inquiry or a more in-depth series of specific questions. The answers received back from a number of clients can be collected, run through affinity (grouped), and weighed to determine which issues may be the most important issues to focus on based on the percentage of times mentioned.

Service-related customer surveys - These can be professionally constructed, distributed, and managed by companies such as Survey Monkey (an on-line cloud-based survey development company). Or they can be created in-house if there are resources available to attend to them professionally and judiciously.

Have engineers check with them during or after service calls - Being that your ground level resources (engineers, admins, technicians, etc.) have daily contact with the clients, teaching them and empowering them to reach out to clients to check for feedback, insights, suggestions, or even complaints could be advantageous and could potentially harvest a good deal of information over relatively short periods of time.

Provide a live chat feature on your web site – An Important consideration for this option is having resources available to both respond to clients leveraging this option on a 24/7 bases and accurately record information from the calls. The accumulated information can be analyzed to determine if there are common themes, issues, or concerns.

Customer Feedback link or button on your web site - This can serve as a somewhat static option that is always available for clients to click on and submit their thoughts. It would be important to monitor the receiving portal or mailbox daily to help assure a timely response to any inquiries made. In addition, the repository of these messages can provide a pool for information that can be analyzed, have metrics derived from and improvement initiative drawn up form.

Focus Groups - These can serve as a more personal and interrogative means of collecting valuable feedback and insight. It provides latitude for questions and answers as well as focusing on specific lines of conversation.

Monitor web site analytics - This is a sometimes-overlooked avenue for harvesting insight on who is visiting your web site, for how long, where they are spending their time, and from what different geographic locations. Some systems can deliver additional metrics pertaining to technology used, personal demographics, and return visits.

Even if you do not use any of the above-mentioned options, you can always create and implement a customer complaint and suggestion system that makes it easy for customers to provide feedback, be it positive or negative.

Oddly enough, as a service manager, I would welcome any negative feedback from a client, primarily because it allows me both the opportunity to resolve the issue for the client who provided the feedback and thus shore up our relationship and it also provides me with insight to an issue that may be systemic and thus impacting other client as well.

I have heard quotes stating that for every client that complaints there are another (20 - 100) that never bothered to mention the same issue. Although receiving a complaint in and of itself is not a good thing, it does however provide an opportunity for improvement overall.

Receiving customer feedback

The goal with receiving customer feedback is to harvest pertinent and honest insights that reflect a general customer consensus. When this information is acted upon it provides an opportunity to increase customer satisfaction and lends to continuous product or service improvement. Impact from customer feedback should be felt all the way back to a product or service's development point or redesign point. This effectively incorporates the voice of the customer into product or service design. Periodically querying the company's complaint department or interviewing front-line salespeople are also avenues for collecting unbiased customer opinion along the lines of "what are they requesting" and "what can we fix or do better".

Regarding methods of meeting customer needs
Although there are several methods by which businesses can meet their customer's needs, I believe that the best methods are those that are based on customer feedback or continuous improvement initiatives and projects. Methodologies such as Six Sigma are good for overall efficiency and reduction of defects. Continuous improvement philosophies such as Kaizen and any related recommendations help to develop a quality focused culture and can also be useful for addressing client needs. Evaluating your specific environment and leveraging any combination of these measures, or others mentioned in this text, should assure some degree of improved customer satisfaction.

Regarding customer loyalty
Knowing your customer, what makes them satisfied as well as what keeps them loyal, is vital to any company that depends on its customer base for revenue.
"The problem is companies are interpreting satisfaction to mean loyalty. Sure, a customer may be satisfied, but if the customer believes she would be equally (or better) satisfied with any other provider, she'll switch." (Coyne, 2009)

A Word on Contracts
For the most part, managers are involved long after the initial sales contract has been negotiated and signed. However, it is particularly important for the service and support manager to know what the contract involves because the obligations related to both service delivery and support fall under his or her care and control.

A contract is a legally enforceable agreement between two or more parties that creates an obligation to do, or not do, particular things. The term "party" can mean an individual person, company, or other legal entity. No matter who the parties are, contracts almost always contain the following essential element and understanding:

Mutual agreement by all the parties. In other words, all parties have a meeting of the minds on a specific subject. Each party either promises to perform an act that the party is not legally required to perform or promises to abstain from performing an act that it is legally entitled to perform. (Reuters, 2018)

It is also important to be in close communications with the sales team – this should include regular meetings and possibly having a technical resource attend initial sales meetings with potential clients to help bridge any technology gaps in the conversation that leads to contractual obligation. This is vital to making sure that what is sold can be achieved and managed from technical and resource perspectives. This curtails possible complications downstream regarding resource availability, capacity, or required skill sets. This is the same reason that the service and support manager needs to be involved in project meetings as well. Resources need to be leveraged across current clients, new clients, and meet current and future project demands. The service and support manager manages these resources.

Service Level Agreements (SLAs)
An especially important component of the service contract should be shared with, understood, and agreed to by most IT service managers are the Service Level Agreements (SLAs). These agreements outline specific parameters regarding service levels and service performance and there are often penalties for not meeting or maintaining the related levels of service. There can also be various levels of service offered (such as standard, premium, 24/7, and priority (1, 2, 3, etc.)); each greater level of service level would of course be

associated with its accompanying cost. Some of the standard items covered in an SLA are response times, availability or "Up-Time", resolution time, quantity/time, as well as rate or percent of resolutions/time and other specific performance focus points.

The SLA holds your company accountable for providing the value it agreed to within the walls of the contract. It may contain verbiage regarding specifics of the service and the associated expected and guaranteed metric for the service level. It may also cover any penalties for not maintaining the agreed upon level of service. It can also be used to bear out your company's performance over time related to the contractual agreements and provide viable information to gage against during daily operations. How well you have historically met the SLAs over time will be an important factor when it becomes time for the client to resign the contract. In some cases, there may be critical impact to your client's business operations or performance if you fail to meet and maintain agreed upon service levels. For example, If Mike's Bicycle Co. has a 1-year contract with your company for providing sprockets; relevant SLAs could be the quantity of sprockets delivered each month or the quality of the sprockets delivered (for example 99.9% defect free), or possibly the response time associated with any issues encountered, such as speed of replacement of the acceptable 0.1% defective sprockets delivered.

The formula for calculating percentage-based SLAs is fairly straightforward and is similar to calculating basic capacity utilization metrics: for example, for the SLA relating to percentage of service tickets closed per day - The number of tickets opened and closed within the SLA threshold (1 day), divided by the number of tickets that were received during that threshold, multiplied by 100 – the resulting number is your percentage. You can match this actual percentage met with the percentage stipulated within the SLA to determine if it was met or not.

One way of continuously monitoring (and being able to rapidly adjust to) SLAs is by creating specific KPIs within your Professional Services Automation (PSA), Customer Relationship Management (CRM), or other business systems that are capable of collecting and reporting on real-time data. You can either run daily metrics reports or set up a dashboard, which would be able to deliver a more dynamic, real-time perspective on how well service performance matches your contractually bound SLAs.

You may also wish to familiarize yourself with any current Operational Level Agreements (OLAs) that your company may have in place – These are internal agreements between departments regarding performance, baselines, and metrics which all support the external SLAs.

Honest Communications

One particular point of failure that you will want to avoid with clients is not maintaining honest and up-front communications – I have heard this referred to as 'Gold Plating' and it is one of the quickest ways of damaging your credibility with clients. I would propose as a critical rule for helping to assure post contract client satisfaction that you never sell a client that which you cannot deliver or support after delivery. Know your abilities, capacity, capabilities, and skill sets well. Understand your metrics comprehensively and manage your commitments honestly.

Capacity Management

For IT service management capacity is generally regarded as the maximum throughput that your service and support teams can manage - for example, the total volume of service and support calls that can be effectively managed within a given time, such as a day. Using this example, the formula for calculating capacity utilization is basically the number of calls that are performed daily divided by the number of calls that can realistically be performed within a day, multiplied by 100. For example, if you know that your team can managed 200 service calls a day and on a given day, they complete 175 service calls, your capacity utilization on that day is 87.5 percent ((175 / 200) x 100). To determine what can realistically be managed in a day you can:

- Pull metrics from data over the course of 6 months or more to determine the number of calls addressed **on the most productive days**
  - Additionally, drill down into that data to determine if there were any special causes or conditions involve with facilitating the optimization **within those days** (such as a resource, a client, a device, platform, day of week, or other)
- Pull metrics from data over the course of 6 months or more to calculate the maximum **hourly** call completions of any time and use it as your base (due to the tight sampling this may generate unrealistic expectations due to normal fluctuations in capacity that can naturally occur over time is not accounted for in the calculations)
- Guestimate based on your qualitative knowledge of your resources and systems (this may not be as accurate as data trending over time)

Note: performing these calculations on your 'average' call performance maximums as opposed to the 'absolute maximum' will yield a more statistically accurate assessment of sustainable capacity utilization over time. This is due to the unlikelihood of your team performing at its absolute maximum 5 days a week every week and the influence of realistic fluctuations in demand, resource availability, or other variables that naturally occur over time.

When dealing with capacity management & efficiency my approach is to keep the 3 variable elements of what I call the **'Capacity Triangle'** in mind (resource efficiency, resource availability, and demand) - a fourth element is 'Time' (which is often held fixed due to contractual SLAs). Think of it as being similar to conditions faced when working with projects where the 3 defining factors are cost, time, and scope - if one of the parameters changes it will impact and require modification of one or both other parameters.

Regarding capacity, the cold, hard fact of the matter is that you cannot have it both ways – that is, you cannot run at near 100% capacity utilization from day to day and still be able to take on a new client (new demand) overnight and be able to accommodate them comfortably, effectively, or efficiently. Nor can you effectively adjust to sudden shifts in demand. However, it is management and leadership's responsibility to stakeholders, staff, and clients to make sure that provisioning for capacity management is both **cost-effective** (avoiding bringing on too many resources to attend to current and projected demand) and **functionally efficient** (avoiding maintaining too few resources and not being able to adopt to sudden increase in demand or being able to efficiently manage the services that were sold and honoring contractual agreements). This becomes a very precarious undertaking due to the inherent dynamic and sometimes unpredictable nature of the three mutable elements that are core to capacity management (the capacity triangle mentioned above).

With all this being said, below are a few steps that I feel can be taken to assist with managing sudden shifts in demand or resources with regards to Capacity Management. Note that these are general, logical suggestions and are not "one-size fits all" solutions. However, the list may contain options that you have never considered before, are germane to your situation, or contains elements that you can work from to build a more personalized solution:

- Plan ahead with current clients with regards to internal changes that they may be planning that will impact your service delivery schema. This can be done via regular change management meetings with them or just established lines for open communication. This allows you time to assess an upcoming change and plan accordingly. This may also open opportunities to sale additional services that are reasonably required to support the proposed changes

- Make sure that current staff ability is optimal (training, certification, knowledge bases, processes, and standards) for them to more readily and comfortably manage increases in demand or reduction in resource availability

- Consistently monitor your ongoing capacity saturation levels to have a sense of how close to saturation you traditionally run. This should be a key KPI and monitored daily and over time to avoid being blindsided by the inadvertent reaching or exceeding a critical resource saturation level

- Extending from the above consideration is knowing how well you are currently meeting all contractual SLAs across all clients. Your company is responsible for maintaining all agreed upon Service Level Agreements and can possibly be fined or otherwise held accountable if they are not met. This element of situational awareness, along with known saturation levels and other KPIs lends greatly to your ability to pro-actively managed staffing and to curtail the possibility of missing an SLA and paying the price (monetarily or in client confidence) for doing so

- Know how long it takes to on-board additional staff if needed for new client demand. This information can tie into project planning, contractual expectations, and known ability to temporarily absorb extended capacity (see next bullet point)

- Hold close relationships with your recruiters so that they are aware of what resource requirements you may have (position descriptions as well as any educational, experience, or certifications needed) to reduce time during the interviewing stages of the recruitment process

- Never run your staff at 100% saturation on a regular basis. In the first place, this may have a deleterious impact on staff morel and performance (see the Yerkes Dodson Law) and secondarily it allows no room to absorb common capacity constraint points such as illness, projects, emergencies, resignations, or terminations. This is where a decision within leadership needs to be made to determine how much capacity should be made available to mitigate the risk of impacting clients due to sudden demand events. Of course, this should be an informed decision based on other measurement based or analysis-based options on this list

- Measure and analyze capacity over time via ongoing data and metrics monitoring and forecasting. This will help you to remain aware of any trending with regards to changes in demand - such as seasonal, holidays, Sales Team performance trending, re-occurring projects, or other reoccurring trends such as across shifts. This may also allow   for   a   degree   of   leveling availability/capability/demand across the peaks and valleys of extended operations.

- Budget accordingly when signing new contracts to absorb the cost of additional resources needed to absorb the new level of demand. This is where the synergy between sales, project management, and service operations becomes essential

- Perform periodic diminished capacity drills in order to determine where the weak points are with regards to managing sudden change - this allows you to make informed decisions on where to shore up your abilities in cases of sudden demand (such as overtime or temp employees to address both availability and capability constraints). This also mentally prepares the staff in the event that such an occasion should arise in the future and allows pre-vetting of the availability of temporary staff with your recruiters

- Absolutely maintain clear and honest consideration and communications with the new or potential client. "Gold Plating" or setting false expectations is one of the best paths for setting yourself up for failure with them - promising one thing while delivering another is an especially bad way to start off any business relationship

Under the umbrella of the premise that all things inside a company are connected, it is important to note that staff training (lends to capability), retention (lends to availability), and engagement (lends to performance) can all impact capacity management. Other high-level impact points are the on boarding of new clients, drastic demand change from current clients, or the loss or non-renewal of a current client contract.

My efficiency deconstruction process

One of the exercises that I perform with regards to examining efficiencies is to systematically inspect 3 areas of concern: <u>the processes</u>, <u>the people</u>, and <u>the tools</u>. This exercise is focused only on areas under my care and control to determine if there are any deficiencies (or conversely area for improvement) related to any individual concern.

For the resources: I examine:

<u>The leadership</u> – Myself, and yes, my boss and his boss if relevant. To most, this may seem a bit odd or unusual; however, it is important to realize that your ability to perform effectively and efficiently is greatly impacted by the person who manages you in a similar way that your staff's performance is impacted by your leadership style, attention, ethics, compassion, and focus. (See 'On Performance' in Chapter 2)

<u>The staff</u> – Examine hiring practices to assure appropriate screening early in the recruiting process. Focus on staff development to assure that they have the proper tools and training. Take steps to assure that they can meet with me and ask questions or express concerns. Provide guidance via astute and data driven personnel reviews, and to manage any performance issues professionally.

It is important to mention that it is advantageous to consider the metal of the people that you use to build your business.

You need to understand a thing to effectively manage a thing.

When a soldier trains, you can see the seriousness, the focus of the training in his expression - strict regimen keeps him aligned and focused on only that which is essential. The same with boxing - that focus, and seriousness, determination and dedication can be seen in their expression- in the old Rocky movies, it was called "Eye of the Tiger".

I will often look for a hint of this "focus", this determination when interviewing new hires; I will often build my interview questions to seek it out.

If you start with good steel, the final blade is destined to be sharp.

The cultural practices – Vital to better manage professionalism, camaraderie, engagement, open communications, and trust. I will pause to emphasize how important it is to address your staff honestly, professionally, and empathetically. Establishing trust with your teams opens doors of communications that are much richer and informative then daily communications established via a casual or tentative day to day rapport. Your team will know when you are straightforward, open, and honest with them and when you are not, so it is critical to remember that once trust is lost – efficiency may fall behind.

The first dysfunction of a team is an absence of trust among team members. Essentially, this stems from their unwillingness to be vulnerable within the group. Team members who are not genuinely open with one another about their mistakes and weaknesses make it impossible to build a foundation for trust." - (Lencioni, 2005)

For programs and tools - Remaining aware of their capabilities to assure that we are using the appropriate tools needed to achieve our goals as well as making sure that we are leveraging the capabilities within our tools to assure that we get the most from our investments

For processes – As mentioned earlier in this text, it is important to periodically review or audit active process and procedure documentation. It may also be necessary to add additional documentation based on operational changes or growth.

Summary

Finally, I will just simply state that regardless of your business venture - if you are the owner of a small grocery store or the CEO of a fortune 500 company, your clients provide the lifeblood that allows your enterprise to live and thrive. You should never lose site of the fact that this is a symbiotic relationship – it is easy for this to occur somewhere along the way, between the thrill of the first sell and when other priorities come into play later. I know for a fact that if leadership does not lose track of how important it is to address the client's needs and is passionate about keeping that understanding attached to the enterprise's mission, vision, and planning, that maintaining a good reputation, satisfied clients, and a prosperous company is all that much more attainable.

Levin J. Allen

CHAPTER 4

On Upper Management

In my opinion, there are only a dozen or so core focal points that need to be on a checklist and attended to for any company, big or small, to start off on the right tracks and maintain an even keel from inception and throughout its existence. Most of these items should be covered in any "Business 101" handbook; however, I will share a few of my insights to augment the standard points and to make the list a bit more comprehensive. The items that are most commonly associated with strategic planning, and should be incorporated into most company's structure, are the following foundation pieces - these you'll find posted on most company web sites and are:

- A company's Vision statement
- A company's Mission statement
- A company's core values
- And in some cases, a company's strategic goals

However, there are other areas of consideration that, when integrated into a company's core structure (and maintained over time), will lend to a company's overall success, sustainability, ability to hire and keep the best resources, its reputation, and its overall ability to succeed and outlive its competitors. I have expanded the traditional list to include the following critical core considerations:

- A clear vision and direction for your company
- Strategic planning that supports your vision

- Tactical planning to accomplish your goals and objectives (derived from your strategic planning)
- Solid, professional staff to carry out you tactical and operational planning
- Code of conduct to guide your staff – (both current and new staff as you grow)
- Inspirational leadership
- An open ear to the voice of your customers
- Always build your next steps and growth on solid foundations
- A well-defined and organized structure
- Well vetted and documented processes and procedures
- A ubiquitous focus on maintaining a positive culture
- Maintaining situational awareness regarding all things that have impact to your company (See SWOT)
- Hardwired mechanisms for continuous improvement
- An understanding of the need to be innovative

Everything from the 2 lists above should be considered and developed by leadership. If rectitude, honor, or a sincere focus on customer needs and company stability are deficient within leadership, it is possible for some or all the items on the latter list to be overshadowed by ulterior objectives that may not be conducive to long-term company success. A few of the objectives and shortcomings were mentioned earlier, such as leadership's focus on its financial performance reporting and appearance of being profitable over the relationships with its clients and staff. (See Balanced Score Cards in Chapter 1)

Strategic Management

Leaders of industries or owners of companies are to some degree responsible for the livelihood of the dedicated employees that work for them – this is inherent in the employment contract – for a person to join your company, to work hard and do one's best in return for a wage and some degree of stability in their personal lives. In this regard, the staff is at the bottom of the list whereas everyone above them (Supervisor, Manager, Director, President, CEO, or other high-level stakeholder) has the power or ability to impact their livelihood adversely or positively. These stakeholders should morally have some direction, some plan for keeping their staff secure, their clients happy, and their companies and enterprises profitable, healthy, and in good standing with society. To this end there is a form of management that can be implemented by all leaders and owners of companies - This is strategic management.

Strategic Management is not extremely hard to define or explain as its name is comprised of only two words and each has a fairly clear and succinct definition in and of itself. Strategic Management is a methodology that is comprised of several specific steps - these steps usually include at least the top 3 items on the following list:

- Vision - where a company sees itself in the future
- Mission - Where a company sees itself currently and its prominent goals
- Core Values - a list of values that the company carries as a flag for both internal and external constituents to see and be aware of
- Broad Strategic Goals - A list of well vetted, high level goals designed to move the company towards its vision

- Action plans - these are derived from the strategic goals and are designed to achieve the company's goals and objectives
- Business Processes - these processes are created to support and define how the action plans are to be carried out consistently over time
- Responsibilities - that are aligned with and assigned to upper management, middle management, supervisors, and staff. This all aligns with the strategic planning associated with the action plans, and business processes developed to facilitate the company's broad strategic goals
- Ongoing situational awareness – regarding not just its financial performance but additionally what its clients and staff think, feel, and experience and how those experiences align with the core mission and vision of the company

Critical Growth Errors

Creating the above-mentioned paths and continually maintaining focus on those considerations can help to set a company on a good course with a solid foundation or "skeleton" if you will. It is the job of leadership to not only create, place, and enforce these elements within a company's structure, but to also assure that the appropriate people, processes, policies, and cultural guidelines are in place to assure the stability and reinforcement of this foundation over time, as the company grows. I have seen first-hand the damage that can be caused when a company grows so fast that leadership fails to realize that there are gaps opening in the very processes, procedures, and policies that led to its growth in the first place. They lose situational awareness of areas that fall under their care and control to manage and the "skeleton" of the company becomes weak or damaged in places. Success can make one complacent or less focused on areas that were once critical for getting a firm footing initially.

If not continually focused and aware, over time leadership can lose its "Eye of the Tiger" so to speak.

Ultimately, sometimes due to waning attention to that which was once vetted, enacted, monitored, and enforced when a company was smaller (and albeit much easier to manage) the missing focus can lead to irreversible cascade failures within its infrastructure that are difficult or near impossible to recover from.

The especially important point that I am trying to make is that **being profitable today as a result of the due diligence of yesterday does not assure smooth sailing tomorrow without that same level of diligence today** – think about it. It may be a more complex function to maintain the same checks, balances, and controls once the company has doubled in size; however, if the focus on and extension of these controls are constant and consistent incrementally over time as the company grows, the task is less daunting, and the risks mitigated. Also, this helps to avoid sudden pitfalls (penalties, unsatisfied clients, regulation violations, compliance issues, staff issues, and most importantly security issues) from subtly taking root and growing within the infrastructure cracks allowed to open due to lack of attention and maintenance during growth.

A few examples of these types of growth error issues are:

- Not maintaining an infrastructure that can support delivering value to your client base as you grow. Deficiencies can occur with staff if capacity and capability management is not monitored and maintained as a company grows. This can be due to not knowing that staff are being tasked with over time as either more clients are acquired, or current client's infrastructures grow. Constant and consistent monitoring of metrics and dashboards can lend to awareness in this regard as can consistently running and monitoring of related reports. Also, deficiencies can be caused by not sufficiently planning and future-proofing critical infrastructure pieces, such as servers, storage, company data backup capability, or even aged computers that may not be able to run the next Operating System or critical business application.

- "Busted pipes" for communication and awareness as you grow – this leads to critical loss of situational awareness. Upper management can keep from losing sight of critical areas as a company grows by putting "repeaters" in place - management personnel to bridge the growing gaps within the growing population and across new areas and departments. These repeaters can also assure that critical policy and procedure related information is being consistently distributed and enforced during growth.

- Forgetting to put the customer first at all levels as you are diverting your attention to internal needs as you adjust to growth.

- Neglecting to disseminate change via change agent hierarchy – transmitting change from upper management to middle management to supervisor to staff. This hierarchy and the associated lines of communications makes it next to impossible for change to not be disseminated to all. Also, the branches for transmission can easily be reviewed via up-to-date company Org Charts. In addition, there should be standard management meetings held to make sure that everyone along the line of dissemination is aware of the specifics of the change. This also allows a venue for Q&A, which can be useful for vetting last minute details, or explaining anything that may be unclear.

- Not keeping up with advancements with technology - technology continues to migrate forward over time and accordingly, clients may want to keep up with the latest technological advancements. An astute client would be following these changes to technology, best practices, and guidelines for future-proofing their company. Not being able to meet or manage requests from clients due to lack of readiness or planning can inhibit new or repeat business – competitors who are ready will receive the business instead. Not being able to meet these requests could be due to lack of skill sets, insufficient technology, lack of ability or knowledge due to insufficient training, or the need to make unplanned and costly infrastructure changes in order to bring the company current or keeping it at the forefront of the technology curve. I have heard a couple of companies refer to this as "Next-Gen" (Next Generation) planning and thinking.

- Loosing track of required certifications - this can sometimes impact your standing with your partners. Partners such as Cisco, Brocade, HP, Dell, and WatchGuard, to name a few, may require that a certain number of technical staff maintain certifications in order to maintain the partnership.

However, you look at it, owners, CEOs, and presidents are the captains of the ships that they lead and are designed to ferry the clients comfortably and securely to where they want to go - that is what the clients pay for. If you are on vacation with your family and you take a 5-day cruise to the Bahamas, all you want to do is sit back and relax - that is what you paid for. You would not understand or appreciate it if you were stuck two miles off shore because the ship neglected to stock enough fuel to make it all the way to the Bahamas, if service was very poor because they were low on staff during your cruise (either they let some go to cut costs or they just quit - it doesn't matter), or if your experience was bad because the crew were not professional and seemed to really not enjoy their jobs. It is the captain and his executive officers' responsibility to assure that all lifeboats are available and in good order and that the kitchen crew is following proper protocol for keeping food safe. It is these same executives on the ship who create the policies and procedures to assure that each passenger who choses their cruise line has a valued and safe experience. Creating the protocol is one step but maintaining it and making sure that it is followed over time and growth is critical.

According to the American Society of quality
"Organizational excellence refers to ongoing efforts to establish an internal framework of standards and processes intended to engage and motivate employees to deliver products and services that fulfill customer requirements within business expectations."
There are many ways to start down the path to organizational excellence; however, they all need to start with and be championed by company leadership.

CHAPTER 5

Regarding the Culture

Because this topic is so very vital to the functionality, stability, and success of a company, I feel that it is important to place a few paragraphs in this book that are focused on the concept of company culture.

I have mentioned culture as it related to various topics at several points in the previous chapters regarding management, staff, and leadership - this was not just a random occurrence. I say this because your company's culture has a great deal to do with regards to everything from the sales of its product or service, throughout support and service delivery, to the point of contract renewals. It also speaks volumes to both internal and external stakeholders and those looking to possibly leverage your goods or services.

A company's culture should be ignited and championed by leadership. I purposely kept the previous sentence short and succinct. In a sense, you can imagine this as being similar to how a mother and/or father shapes the character of their children as they grow and develop. If a child is cared for well and taught the right things - to be honest, honorable, thrifty, benevolent, polite, brave, focused, and loyal - the odds are that he or she is far more likely do well at whatever phase they are in life and less likely to end up in jail, on drugs, or grow into adulthood with a terrible past and heading for no certain future. It is also likely that those who know, or know of, this child will develop an opinion of the child's character, inclinations, and upbringing. "Oh, there goes the Smith child -

be careful because he is always up to no good. You can just tell that he was not raised right". The reputation of the child is associated with his parental management. This reflects how the reputation of your company can be impacted by the staff that you "raise" – especially when they are the "face" of the company when working directly with your clients.

I take this same "Parental" approach with my staff, especially young, green staff as they come on-board. I not only try to impress upon them that due diligence pays off but try to lead by example as well. One of the reasons that I do this is because I was fortunate enough to have had exceptionally good managers and bosses at the start of my career and learned early the benefits of good communication, good treatment, good guidance, and good leadership – to this day I think very highly of these individuals. Whenever anyone has a manager or boss who is communicative, honest, genuine, and does not curse at, berate, or yell at them; but still professionally holds them accountable and works to keep them empowered and on the proper path - it both raises their comfort level at work and garners greater engagement and productivity from them. I will emphasize that not being a hatchet man is fine; however, at the same time a manager needs to hold his staff accountable as well as direct, guide, and develop them - similar to the parent scenario that I mentioned earlier. This is a knack, a balance that is hard to achieve, especially given the variety of personalities and personal styles that a manager needs to contend with over time.

In this sense, yes, managers and bosses need to set the tone when it comes to developing and maintain a positive, constructive, and synergistic culture. I have a saying that I have shared with all my teams: "<u>Who we are is us - how we treat each other and how we work together as a team. That defines our culture and that greatly contributes to our success</u>."

If you check back to the beginning of chapter one, I mentioned 6 steps that I have developed for on boarding to a new position in order to bring myself up to speed and achieve efficiency within a relatively short period of time. Note that the second step is to build team dynamics (trust, communications, connections, synergy, and action).

Patrick Lencioni writes in his book 'The 5 Dysfunctions of a Team':
"<u>The first dysfunction is an absence of trust among team members. Essentially, this stems from their unwillingness to be vulnerable within the group. Team members who are not genuinely open with one another about their mistakes and weaknesses make it impossible to build a foundation for trust</u>."

I agree with him and have actually worked with this concept over time to bear it out. It is also true that moral leadership inspires ethical behavior. This is something that just about any of us can identify with - think back to the bosses that you have had in the past. Which inspired you? Which did you want to emulate? And which do you think back about with a sense of dread, frustration, or anger. And even more profound, how would you like to be remembered by your team members as they move through their careers? If you are thinking as an inspiration, then your hearts in the right place. If you are thinking that you really do not care, then maybe you should consider a career change to one that is not responsible for the growth and development of other human beings.

I had a discussion with the CEO of a large and growing company regarding making sure that voids in process, procedure, standards, and culture do not open up during times of company growth and the potentially disastrous outcomes of not being attentive to managing elements such as culture as a company grows. He correctly pointed out that you can teach your staff something beneficial today; however, over time those useful and productive guidelines tend to get lost and ultimately forgotten. This is where the conversation became focused on how to best mitigate that risk. One solution I suggested is to "ingrain" the philosophies related to maintaining a positive culture into the staff from on-boarding to the time that someone leaves the company. This can be done through constant and ever-present messages that convey the company's stance on culture as well as leadership's determination to champion and enforce maintaining a positive culture every day. This highlights the critical requirement of leadership to never allow the customs and norms of the company to drift backwards over time or become diluted during growth. This is a conscience effort and does take dedication to maintain. However, considering the benefits (happier and more comfortable staff, company reputation, the ability to attract and hold onto the best talent, more efficient operations, and satisfied clients - to name a few), it becomes an element that good leadership should choose to pick up and carry because they believe that it is worth the effort.

By the end of the conversation, we both agreed that although it is good and wise for leadership to take the time to develop and implement effective and beneficial business cultural guidelines and codes of conduct, is equally critical for leadership to maintain and incorporate those philosophies, guidelines, methodologies, and accommodations within the company over time. If not, the best that you can say that was achieved was a good "temporary work around", as opposed to a real solution that the company can continue to benefit from.

The development of a quality culture

Other mechanisms that can be leveraged to assure that not only company culture, but processes, procedures, and standards are maintained over time are:

A written and ubiquitous **Code of Conduct** - This can be drawn up in a day by leadership focusing on what they envision as the qualities they wish to introduce to, and ingrain within the company. This includes what is experienced internally as well as what is experienced externally by clients.

Cultural transmitters or "repeaters" - These are the managers and supervisors who fit between leadership and ground level staff; their goal is to discuss, coordinate with, and receive the "commandments" from leadership and convey them succinctly and continuously to staff - praising adherence and correcting recalcitrance or non-compliance.

Focus during recruitment on hire managers who can serve as effective components of **ethical leadership.** This assures that the hands that receive the orders and instructions from management are capable to conveying them comprehensively and in a committed fashion - to assist with them becoming the norm. If they cannot lead by example and follow the rules that they are responsible for conveying - than those rules cannot be effectively transmitted to the staff.

Vetting quality of character, maturity, and professionalism as early as the first interview for staff - This is something that I mentioned a few times earlier as I honestly believe this to be a critical consideration if you are looking to both build and maintain your culture. The wrong pieces can cause disruptions and setbacks and can ultimately cost more time, effort, energy, and expense to correct. Managing this risk early can save all stakeholders involved quite a bit of grief.

Defining and establishing the company's **organizational context** - An organization's context is its business environment. It includes all the internal and external factors and conditions that affect its products and services, have an influence on its Quality Management Systems, and are relevant to its purpose and strategic direction.

Leadership **becoming an advocate of quality** - Any profound or lasting change within a company needs to be championed, supported, and maintained by leadership - these are the Owners, the CEOs, the Presidents, and the like.

Bring the **service staff closer to the client perspective** via training and awareness - empathy and awareness can be generated simply by educating your staff on elements of quality, value, how client satisfaction benefits the company and themselves, as well as how clients see things from their perspective.

Replace the act of berating with praise - Manage staff by micromanaging only when needed and praising when it is not. Helping to develop an individual's dignity, sense of worth, and capacity via clear instructions, guidance, and professional treatment lends greatly to a quality culture.

Everything is connected

In the end it is vital to bear in mind that within a company, everything is connected - Staff morale, performance, management style, leadership style, and client satisfaction to name a few. I have an analogy where I compare a company to a clock - there are big gears, medium gears, and small gears however, all the gears need to turn smoothly and work together seamlessly to deliver the one thing that the client has paid for and expects - the correct time.

CHAPTER 6

Japanese concepts and methodologies

A Brief History of Quality Focus in Japan

It would be hard for me to complete this book without acknowledging the contributions of Japanese culture, innovators, and philanthropist to the development of many of the quality management, improvement methodologies, and philosophies used today.

Most people do not realize that after World War II, a large portion of Japan's industry, which was previously focused on producing war time materials, had to convert to focus on the production of consumer goods. This was an effort to reestablish viability of its infrastructure and an attempt to strengthen its post-war economy.

Those of you who are old enough may recall that around that time (Mid 40s to early 60s) the term "Made in Japan" was synonymous with 'poorly made' or 'cheap' products. Because of this Japans attempts to compete in the international marketplace in an attempt to boost its economy was disastrous to say the least. It was not until the late 1940s that Japan came to realize that quality, not price (cheaply made and sold), was the key to competing on the international stage. It was during this time that several Japanese leaders invited W. Edward Deming to visit Japan and share his views on quality. At the time, Deming had developed groundbreaking ideas regarding quality management and attempted to share his ideas with US corporations and manufacturers. However, during those post war years, US corporations were basking in their post-war opulence and did not see any benefit in focusing on quality, thus Deming and his ideas were not received well in the US. Due to this ubiquitous snubbing of his ideas in the US, Deming accepted the invitation from Japan's industrialists, who recognized his ideas and embraced them whole heartedly and with open arms.

This was the turning point for Japan, from this point forward, companies such as Toyota, Mitsubishi, Toshiba, Kawasaki, and others were able to significantly increase quality with their products, reduce production times, and reduce waste. Because of these manufacturing and production improvements, Japan became extremely competitive within the international marketplace. I mention all this because today Japan sits very prominently on the world stage regarding innovation, trade, quality, and commerce; however, it was able to rise to its current level of competitiveness by seeking out and leveraging best practices, focusing on quality controls, and by paying attention to, (as well as developing ways to) achieve customer wants and needs cost effectively.

Side Note – to point out the costs of not being innovative and missing opportunities: By the end of the 1970s, America was suffering from a quality crisis and struggling in the international marketplace – partially due to competition from Japan. By the 1980s, leading industrialists in the United States were facing similar quality related issues to what their Japanese counterparts had been experiencing in the late 1940s. Knowing of the substantial impact that Deming's teachings had had on Japanese productivity, US corporations began to reach out to Deming for his advice as well – the same advice that he had offered them some 40 years earlier, before going to Japan, but at that time they were not interested. (Goetsch, 2012)

Finally, I'll mention that during the time between the 1940 and the 1980, Japanese businessmen and industrialist developed many of the quality management, statistical quality control, and continuous improvement methodologies and tools that remain in use today. Below I have listed a few of the tools that I am most familiar with. I am only providing a brief overview of each, so please take the time to research any/all of the terms to become better acquainted with their concepts as many may be beneficial to know and understand.

Japanese businesses philosophies:

- **Genchi Genbutsu** (by Taiichi Ohno) - To go to the actual place in order to determine what an issue may be – essentially, instead of stopping at a question mark or uncertainty go and see

- **Kaizen** (by Masaaki Imai) - Continuous improvement of all things at all levels at all times. Improvement efforts can range from small and incremental to large initiatives or projects and can be suggested by anyone in the company. All insights can potentially provide value and anyone's observations can potentially capture unique insight, depending on your area of work, focus, or expertise. According to an article posted in Inc. Magazine - Toyota employees speak up when they see room for improvement on or off the assembly line. The company reports that their 67,000 employees submit over 700,000 suggestions for internal improvement each year, about 99% of which are implemented. For Toyota, small improvements make all the difference. Every employee is not only able to stop the line or make a suggestion, they have a responsibility to Toyota to actively improve all the time. (Chen, 2016)

- **Kano Model** (by Professor Noriaki Kano) - Displays the correlation between quality of function and client satisfaction. This model is based primarily on 3 areas of quality (performance, expected quality, and exciters) and the entire model is continuously being driven forward by both competition and innovation

- **Omotenashi** (おもてなし) – This is a Japanese phrase that means 'Hospitality' or 'To accommodate'. It is a selfless form of hospitality and a practice of going above and beyond to welcome guests and to ensure that they are happy. It has also been leveraged to accommodate clients. It is an important part of the Japanese culture and it involves the subjugation of self in service to a guest, without being "servile". Anticipating needs is at the heart of the concept

- **Poka-yoke** (by Shigeo Shingo) – literal translation of the words: "Avoid Mistakes". This is a Japanese business (primarily manufacturing) philosophy that focus on the prevention of mistakes or on issues avoidance. It is akin to Kaizen whereas it focuses on improvement based on observation and paying attention to issues within operations that can lead to production errors or defects

- **Heijunka** (平準化) - A Japanese word that means 'Leveling'. It is traditionally associated with process improvement initiatives that focus on the reduction of waste by using data, metrics, or historical trending to better understand patterns related to customer demand and "Leveling" production or inventory accordingly. However, I have come to associate this term with IT service capacity management by understanding both the impact and recovery steps related to sudden capacity demand or sudden resource ability / availability changes

- **Jiko kaizen** (自己改善) – This is a Japanese phrase that is usually associated with personal fitness; however, I have adopted it to represent my personal improvement philosophy. It is directed inward to one's personal self, as a resource for a business, as opposed to the business itself. Another way to state this is "Always improve yourself - いつも自分自身を改善 - Itsumo jibun jishin o kaizen"

- **5S** (a component of Kaizen) that primarily focuses on 5 elements for order and structure within a manufacturing arena. However, I feel that most of these components can be leveraged within the service management arena as well. The 5 Ss stand for:
  - <u>**Seiri**</u> (整理) To Sort – To separate that which is useful from that which is useless
  - <u>**Seiton**</u> (整頓) To Store – To make sure that everything is kept in its place
  - <u>**Seiso**</u> (清楚) Shine – To keep both your equipment and your work area neat and clean
  - <u>**Seiketsu**</u> (清潔にする) To Standardize – To create and maintain Standard Operating Procedures
  - <u>**Shitsuke**</u> (しつけ) To Sustain Order- To assure that rules, policies, and procedures are adhered to

- 人生の教訓 注意を払う – This is a Japanese phrase that I put together a while ago and reference often. I'm adding it here as I feel that it fits this topic. It translates to: "Pay attention to Life's Lessons" (Jinsei no kyōkun chūiwoharau)

I mention the following because I feel that it is relevant to leadership:

The Bushido Code: (The Eight Virtues of the Samurai)
(武士道コード) (by Nitobe Inazō)
    I. Rectitude or Justice
    II. Courage
    III. Benevolence or Mercy
    IV. Politeness
    V. Honesty and Sincerity
    VI. Honor
    VII. Loyalty
    VIII. Character and Self-Control

Sun Tzu sayings on...:
Directions - If words of command are not clear and distinct and orders are not thoroughly understood, the general is to blame. But if his orders ARE clear, and the soldiers nevertheless disobey, then it is the fault of the soldiers or their officers

Leadership - A leader leads by example not by force

Strategy and Tactics - Strategy without tactics is the slowest route to victory. Tactics without strategy is the noise before defeat

Victory - A skilled commander seeks victory from the situation and does not demand it of his subordinates

CHAPTER 7

Summary

Everything stems from good leadership

Starting, owning, or being a stakeholder in a company requires great insight, forethought, and understanding of all of the constituent components, concerns, influencers, and impactors, both internal and external, related to the undertaking. It also comes with great responsibility. If your honest desire is for your company or investment to grow and to remain profitable over time it is absolutely vital that you have taken the time to understand what traditionally and consistently has (a) caused companies to fail and to avoid those recognized pitfalls at all costs and to (b) understand what available tools, methodologies, best practices, philosophies, and proven initiatives have historically and consistently lent to order, growth, and prosperity.

To summarize and recap - the core areas of concern for any company owner, leader, or top-level executive should be:
- Client satisfaction
- Maintaining a quality culture
- Strategic Planning
- Situational Awareness
- Continuous Improvement
- Pursuing Company Profitability and Success (but not at the cost of any of the aforementioned items)

Creating a quality culture requires involvement from the top executives by way of their vision, direction, and understanding of the value-add of having satisfied customers as well as understanding why employees need to be involved, engaged, and empowered.

Creating total quality in an organization encompasses a focus on continuous improvement and includes items such as involved leadership, clear organizational values, planning and direction, engaged employees, and even cultural transmitters to assure proliferation of both strategic goals and culture quality.

A good manager should not only know the techniques, relationships, strategies, best practices, and processes – he or she should also know how they all fit together.

Within the walls of a successful company - everything is connected

Appendix A

Inspirational Leadership Quotes

"Success is not the key to happiness. Happiness is the key to success. If you love what you are doing, you will be successful." - **Albert Schweitzer**

"I have learned that people will forget what you said, people will forget what you did, but people will never forget how you made them feel." - **Maya Angelou**

"Whether you think you can or you think you can't, you're right." - **Henry Ford**

"Well done is better than well said" – **Benjamin Franklin**

"Life is 10 percent what happens to me and 90 percent of how I react to it." - **Charles Swindoll**

"The two most important days in your life are the day you are born and the day you find out why." - **Mark Twain**

"To handle yourself, use your head; to handle others, use your heart." - **Eleanor Roosevelt**

"When you cease to dream you cease to live." - Malcolm Forbes

"Do or do not. There is no try." - **Yoda**

"I have missed more than 9000 shots in my career. I have lost almost 300 games. Twenty-six times I have been trusted to take the game winning shot and missed. I have failed over and over and over again in my life. And that is why I succeed." - **Michael Jordan**

"Strive not to be a success, but rather to be of value." - **Albert Einstein**

"Live as if you were to die tomorrow. Learn as if you were to live forever." - **Mahatma Gandhi**

"I am not a product of my circumstances. I am a product of my decisions." - **Stephen Covey**

"Until you value yourself, you won't value your time. Until you value your time, you will not do anything with it." - **M. Scott Peck**

"Don't judge each day by the harvest you reap but by the seeds that you plant." -**Robert Louis Stevenson**

"Build your own dreams, or someone else will hire you to build theirs." - **Farrah Gray**

"A person who never made a mistake never tried anything new." - **Albert Einstein**

"When one door of happiness closes, another opens, but often we look so long at the closed door that we do not see the one that has been opened for us." - **Helen Keller**

"Be yourself. Everyone else is already taken." - **Oscar Wilde**

"Don't cry because it's over, smile because it happened." - **Dr. Seuss**

"The only person you are destined to become is the person you decide to be." -**Ralph Waldo Emerson**

"Believe you can and you're halfway there." - **Theodore Roosevelt**

"If you want to be happy, set a goal that commands your thoughts, liberates your energy, and inspires your hopes."- **Andrew Carnegie**

"Your most unhappy customers are your greatest source of learning." – **Bill Gates**

"Anyone can achieve their fullest potential, who we are might be predetermined, but the path we follow is always of our own choosing. We should never allow our fears or the expectations of others to set the frontiers of our destiny. Your destiny can't be changed but, it can be challenged. Every man is born as many men and dies as a single one." **- Martin Heidegger**

My poetry and thoughts:

Boundless
THE ENERGY IS ENDLESS FOR CREATION AND FOR ALL THINGS.
OUR MINDS, HEARTS, AND BELIEFS CREATE THE MANUFACTURING
ENVIRONMENT FOR CREATING THAT WHICH CAN BE.
OUR IMAGINATIONS ARE THE BLUEPRINTS FOR CONSTRUCTION
AND OUR DETERMINATION AND TENACITY IS THE FUEL USED TO GET THE JOB
DONE.
KNOW THIS. BELIEVE THIS. AND YOU CAN ACHIEVE ANYTHING.
— LEVIN ALLEN

Harmony with today
ALWAYS BE YOUR VERY BEST TODAY AND YOU ARE WELL ON YOUR WAY
TO BEING YOUR VERY BEST TOMORROW.
ALWAYS EMBRACE THE GOOD AND BAD, HOT AND COLD, UPS AND DOWNS OF
TODAY AND YOU WILL ALWAYS BE IN HARMONY WITH TOMORROW.
GOVERN YOUR PASSIONS, DESIRES, FEARS, AND ANXIETIES AND CONTROL
THEM OR ELSE THEY WILL CONTROL YOU AND YOUR FUTURE - EITHER YOU
LEAD OR THEY DO.
FIND PEACE IN YOUR TODAY AND YOU ARE ASSURED A PEACEFUL TOMORROW
AND WILL ALWAYS LOOK BACK ON A PEACEFUL PAST.
— LEVIN ALLEN

Appendix B

14 Teachings of Sun Tzu and how I relate them to modern day business practices

Sun Tzu says:

Quote: "When troops flee, are insubordinate, or are routed in battle - it is the fault of the general"
How I relate it to modern day Business: This is similar to failures with managerial and upper management leadership, it reflects the results (staff leaving the company or not performing optimally when needed) of poor leadership.

Quote: "If instructions are not clear and commands not explicit, it is the commander's fault. But if the orders are clear it is the fault of the subordinate that the instructions are not followed".
How I relate it to modern day Business: This is similar to both bad communications and the lack of availability of clear, current, and specific processes, procedures, and policies – these are the documents that contain the clear instructions that all are to follow.

Quote: "There are five fundamental factors in war: Weather, terrain, leadership, military doctrine, and most importantly- moral influence".
How I relate each to modern day Business:
These five factors roughly translate in business to:
Weather – equates to the business environment of today, a company's external environment - relating to competition, decline in sales, environmental impact, public perception, and

so on- it represents external forces that are beyond your immediate control, can change suddenly, and when change does occur you need to be prepared

Terrain – this equates to technology changes, platform changes, demand changes, client expectation changes, and so on – these aspects represent the terrain of business today

Leadership – This is the same with business today as it was when written about war – and denotes the impact of leadership as a fundamental factor of a business and whether its goals are won or lost. Winning or losing depends on leadership's ability to maintain strong and competent staff (troops) as well as sound tactical planning (doctrine).

Military doctrine – In business today, this is equivalent to a company's written and conveyed policies, processes, procedures, mission and vision statements, and strategic plans

Moral influence - This is a very important consideration as there can be either morally good or bad leaders; leaders that want to build and promote positive impact on things around them or leaders that want to plunder as much as possible at any cost everything around them – it denotes the impact of moral and ethical leadership and determines in which philosophical house you stand.

Quote: "The way a wise general can achieve greatness beyond ordinary men is through foreknowledge"
How I relate it to modern day Business: In today's business arena this would be similar to situational awareness and a leader's ability to maintain astute awareness, forecast accurately, and to strategically leverage the information to the company's betterment.

Quote: "Know your enemy and know yourself and in 100 battles you will never be in peril".

How I relate it to modern day Business: This would be equivalent to knowing your competitions strengths and weaknesses as well as knowing those of your own company and continuously leveraging that insight to your company's advantage.

Quote: "The winning army realizes the conditions for victory first, then fights - the losing army fights first, then seeks victory".

How I relate it to modern day Business: I have always associated this insight to service delivery whereas both myself and my engineers always "measure twice to need only to cut once" – this means knowing the facts before we act and being aware of the full impact of our actions.

Quote: "To win 100 battles is not the height of skill - To subdue the enemy without fighting is".

How I relate it to modern day Business: I have always equated this to the concept of lean - (doing the best (winning) more efficiently and at less cost and with less effort)

Quote: "Avoid what is strong. Attack what is weak".

How I relate it to modern day Business: In business operations this can be analogous to leveraging the Pareto Principle in order to target the areas that will grant you the most gain for your efforts. Resolving strategically where 80 percent of the issues are related to 20 percent of the problems – attack the 20 percent to remove the related 80 percent.

Quote: "It is essential for victory that generals are unconstrained by their leaders".

How I relate it to modern day Business: This involves trust, empowerment, and the lack of micromanagement with regards to managers and company leadership.

Quote: "It is more important to out-think your enemy than to outfight him".
How I relate it to modern day Business: In business this is just the application of the old adage "work smarter, not harder".

Quote: "There are some armies that should not be fought - Some ground that should not be contested".
How I relate it to modern day Business: In business, this is the bases of strategic planning when it comes to setting your projects, initiatives, and strategic goals allowing you to focus your efforts on that which is attainable as opposed to that which is doubtful. It is awareness of your capabilities as well as your current limitations.

Quote: "No nation has ever benefited from prolonged war".
How I relate it to modern day Business: No company ever benefits from prolonged dissatisfaction (with its clients, staff, or stakeholders)

Quote: "In war, numbers alone confer no advantage - Do not advance relying on sheer military power".
How I relate it to modern day Business: Ample resources without leadership and strategic planning denotes no real advantage.

Quote: "Let your plans be as dark as night - Then strike like a thunderbolt".
How I relate it to modern day Business: All planning for new product or service offerings should be kept out of the purview of your competition until the time they are to be revealed

Bibliography

Web Sites:

Agrawal, A. (2016, May 18). How Unhappy Employees Can Cost Your Company Millions. Retrieved December 19, 2017, from https://www.huffingtonpost.com/aj-agrawal/how-unhappy-employees-can_b_10029960.html

Air University (2014, February 11). Leadership Principles. Retrieved January 06, 2018, from http://www.au.af.mil/au/awc/awcgate/usmc/leadership.htm

Ashford Global IT (2016, November 11). The Four P's of ITIL® Service Design. Retrieved January 22, 2018, from https://www.ashfordglobalit.com/training-blog/itil-tips-and-training/the-four-ps-of-itil-service-design.html

Chen, W. (2016, October 6). This Japanese Business Practice Will Completely Change the Quality of Your Work. Retrieved January 24, 2018, from https://www.inc.com/walter-chen/this-japanese-philosophy-will-be-your-most-powerful-tool-for-success.html

Dreeke, R. (2016, June 01). How To Get People To Like You: 7 Ways From An FBI Behavior Expert. Retrieved January 28, 2018, from https://www.bakadesuyo.com/2014/10/how-to-get-people-to-like-you/

Gallup, I. (2015, April 08). Employees Want a Lot More From Their Managers. Retrieved December 12, 2017, from http://news.gallup.com/businessjournal/182321/employees-lot-managers.aspx

Jacques , T. (2014, June 11). The Boss Didn't Say Good Morning - vidéo Dailymotion. Retrieved February 02, 2018, from http://www.dailymotion.com/video/x1z4ex3

Japan Today (2014, May 03). The business of 'omotenashi'. Retrieved December 14, 2017, from https://japantoday.com/category/features/opinions/the-business-of-omotenashi

Kanebo Cosmetics Inc. (2015). Omotenashi – The spirit of Japanese hospitality. Retrieved from http://www.kanebo.com/beautyadvice/omotenashi/omotenashi.html

Marines, U. (2013, March 15). Copeland's Assault Course instills combat mindset. Retrieved January 06, 2018, from http://www.mcrdsd.marines.mil/News/News-Article-Display/Article/529707/copelands-assault-course-instills-combat-mindset/

Masood, A. (n.d.). Notes on Basics of Business Psychology. Retrieved January 28, 2018, from https://www.scribd.com/doc/16465515/Notes-on-Basics-of-Business-Psychology

Merhar, C. (n.d.). Employee Retention - The Real Cost of Losing an Employee. Retrieved February 24, 2018, from https://www.zanebenefits.com/blog/bid/312123/employee-retention-the-real-cost-of-losing-an-employee

Mitsubishi. (n.d.). Origin. Retrieved February 06, 2018, from https://www.mitsubishi.com/e/history/

OSHA. (n.d.). UNITED STATES DEPARTMENT OF LABOR. Retrieved February 10, 2018, from https://www.osha.gov/as/opa/worker/employer-responsibility.html

Reuters, T. (n.d.). Contracts Basics. Retrieved January 20, 2018, from http://smallbusiness.findlaw.com/business-contracts-forms/contracts-basics.html

Ryan, L. (n.d.). 'Talent Retention' Problems? Hint: Your Culture Is Broken. Retrieved December 19, 2017, from https://www.forbes.com/sites/lizryan/2016/10/02/why-healthy-companies-dont-fret-about-talent-retention/#10c025446277

(Salesforce.com, 2017)
Salesforce. (n.d.). Home. Retrieved January 12, 2018, from https://www.desk.com/success-center/customer-service-principles

Voices, V. (2017, February 28). Don't Be Surprised When Your Employees Quit. Retrieved October 12, 2017, from https://www.forbes.com/sites/valleyvoices/2017/02/22/dont-be-surprised-when-your-employees-quit/#180ec772325e

Alliance of Automobile Manufacturers (n.d.). Innovation. Retrieved January 19, 2018, from https://autoalliance.org/innovation/

BOOKS:
Coyne, K. (2009, June 19). The customer satisfaction survey snag. Retrieved from http://www.businessweek.com/managing/content/jun2009/ca20090619_272945.htm

Goetsch, D., & Davis, S. (2012). Quality management for organizational excellence. Prentice Hall.

Kumar, D. (2013). Report on leadership style of bill gates. Retrieved from http://www.scribd.com/doc/16315025/Leadership-Style-of-Billgates

Pyzdek, T., & Keller, P. A. (2010). The Six Sigma handbook a complete guide for green belts, black belts, and managers at all levels. New York: McGraw-Hill.

Quality Management for Organizational Excellence – Introduction to Total Quality 7th Ed.
ISBN: 978-0-13-255898-3
Authors: D Goetsch and S Davis

Thomas (2002) Introduction to Conflict Management (Kenneth W. Thomas, 2002, CPP Inc.)

Tzu, S., & Giles, L. (2012). The art of war. New York: Barnes & Noble.

EBOOKS:
Daft, R. L. (02/2009). Management [VitalSource Bookshelf version]. Retrieved from https://bookshelf.vitalsource.com/books/1111440018

Goetsch, D. L., Davis, S. (01/2012). Quality Management for Organizational Excellence: Introduction to Total Quality, 7th Edition [VitalSource Bookshelf version]. Retrieved from https://bookshelf.vitalsource.com/books/9781256643289

Tzu, S., & Giles, L. (2012) The Art of War ISBN: 978-1-4351-4102-5 Nook ed.

P Lencioni The five dysfunctions of a team: a leadership fable. ISBN: 0-7879-6075-6 Nook ed.
Author:

Other

BUS4101_Quality Management © 2009 South University

ABOUT THE AUTHOR

Levin Allen has over 17 years of IT service delivery and support, infrastructure and technology support, and IT staff management experience. During his time within IT Management his focus was also placed on examining and studying IT Management tools and methodologies and the issues related to service delivery and service support. He has gained a firm understanding of the importance of leadership, client satisfaction, continuous improvement, data analysis, situational awareness, and ethical behavior within the context of IT management and the impact that these aspects have on company success and revenue. Along with his Bachelor of Science in Information Technology Degree, he is Six Sigma Green Belt (Quality Management) and ITIL (Service Delivery) certified and very experienced with managing staff, SLAs, Root Cause Analysis, and strategic planning. He is most known for being Efficient, Ethical, Honest and Professional.

<<<<>>>>

www.ingramcontent.com/pod-product-compliance
Lightning Source LLC
Chambersburg PA
CBHW060042210326
41520CB00009B/1230